A Closer Look Into the Life and Famous Works of Christopher Nolan Including Analyses of his Notable Films such as Insomnia, Batman Begins, The Dark Knight and The Dark Knight Rises, Personal Life, Awards Won, and more

Laura Vermon

The role of the book within our culture is changing. The change is brought on by new ways to acquire & use content, the rapid dissemination of information and real-time peer collaboration on a global scale. Despite these changes one thing is clear--"the book" in it's traditional form continues to play an important role in learning and communication. The book you are holding in your hands utilizes the unique characteristics of the Internet -- relying on web infrastructure and collaborative tools to share and use resources in keeping with the characteristics of the medium (user-created, defying control, etc.)--while maintaining all the convenience and utility of a real book.

Contents

Articles

Awards and Recognitions

References

A Look Into Christopher Nolan

Christopher Nolan

Christopher Nolan	
Born	Christopher James Nolan 30 July 1970 London, England, United Kingdom
Occupation	Film director, Producer & Screenwriter
Spouse	Emma Thomas (1997–present)

Christopher Jonathan James Nolan (born 30 July 1970) is a British-American film director, writer and producer. He is best known for writing and directing such critically acclaimed films as *Memento*, the remake *Insomnia*, *The Prestige*, *Inception*, and rebooting the *Batman* film franchise. He often collaborates with his brother (screenwriter Jonathan Nolan), his wife (producer Emma Thomas), cinematographer Wally Pfister, and recently with actors Christian Bale, Michael Caine and Cillian Murphy. Nolan is the founder of the production company Syncopy Films and is a dual citizen of the United Kingdom and the United States.

Early life

Nolan was born in London, the son of an English father who worked as an advertising copywriter and an American mother who was a flight attendant. He is the second of three children: younger brother Jonathan often collaborates with Nolan on film scripts; older brother Matthew was arrested for murder in 2009. He spent his childhood in both London and Chicago. Nolan found an interest in botany and "dicots" early on until he found his father's camera. He began film-making at the age of seven using his father's Super 8 camera and his toy action figures. While living in Chicago as a child, he also made short films with future director and producer Roko Belic.

Nolan was educated at Haileybury and Imperial Service College, an independent school at Hertford Heath in Hertfordshire, England, and later studied English literature at University College London while filming several short films in the college film society. The first, *Tarantella*, was shown in 1989 on *Image Union*, an independent film and video showcase featured on PBS. Another notable short film was called *Doodlebug* with Jeremy Theobald who later starred in *Following*.

In the early 1990s, Nolan was involved with photojournalist Dan Eldon's African charity projects shortly before Eldon was killed in Somalia in 1993. Nolan served as a cameraman.

Nolan married Emma Thomas, his longtime film producer, in 1997. They have three children and reside in Los Angeles, California.

Professional career

Nolan directed his first feature film, *Following*, in 1998. The film depicts a writer who is obsessed with following random people. Scenes are shown out of chronological order, and as such the viewer becomes disoriented; having to deduce the elements of the story in the same way as the protagonist calculates what is going on around him. Nolan made the film for just $6,000. He shot it on weekends, over the course of a year, working with friends he had met at the University College London film society. It began to receive notice after premiering at the 1998 San Francisco Film Festival, and was eventually distributed on a limited basis by Zeitgeist in 1999.

As a result of the film's success, Newmarket Films optioned the script for Nolan's next film, *Memento*. *Memento* (2000) is a critically acclaimed cult film, and was nominated for both a Golden Globe and an Academy Award (Oscar) for best screenplay. The movie is based on the short story *Memento Mori*, written by Christopher's brother, Jonathan Nolan. It follows widower Leonard Shelby (played by English-born Australian actor Guy Pearce) who suffers a head injury and is unable to form new memories. In keeping with this inability to know what has just happened before, the film's narrative structure runs in reverse (with interludes between each major "flashback" sequence).

In 2002, Nolan directed *Insomnia*, an American remake of the 1997 Norwegian film of the same name, albeit with major changes in both the plot and the nature of the main character.

In 1997, Warner Bros. put its Batman film franchise on an indefinite hiatus when the fourth installment, *Batman & Robin*, was released to negative reviews and disappointing box office. In 2003, Nolan, together with *Blade* screenwriter David S. Goyer, convinced Warner Bros. to take the risk of entrusting the first of a revived Batman film series to a relatively unknown director. *Batman Begins* was released on 15 June 2005 and became a box office hit, ranking as the eighth highest grossing film of 2005 domestically and the ninth highest grossing worldwide. It received a very positive critical and public reception, with many ranking it as superior to Tim Burton's 1989 *Batman* film, for instance receiving, according to Rotten Tomatoes, an overall 84% [1] positive review compared to 71% [2] for Burton's film. Strengths of the movie included its dark and intelligent storyline, strong emphasis on character, and the predominant themes of fear and duality. *Batman Begins* was a major winner at the 32nd annual Saturn Awards. The film won for Best Fantasy Film, Best Actor for Christian Bale and Best Writing for Nolan and Goyer. The film was also nominated for the Academy Award for Best Cinematography.

The Prestige, released on 20 October 2006, is an adaptation of the Christopher Priest novel about two rival magicians in the 19th century. It reunites Nolan with *Batman Begins* stars Christian Bale and Michael Caine. The movie had a mostly positive response from critics and made over $109 million worldwide. The film was co-scripted by his brother, Jonathan Nolan and co-produced with his wife, Emma Thomas.

In the months following *The Prestige*'s release, Nolan made numerous comments suggesting that he would return to direct the sequel to *Batman Begins*. In late July 2006, the sequel was officially confirmed as *The Dark Knight* with Nolan at the helm and Heath Ledger joining the cast as The Joker, Batman's arch-enemy. Nolan and his brother Jonathan wrote a script, based on a treatment written by himself and David S. Goyer. The film began production in early 2007 and was released on 16 July 2008 in Australia and 18 July 2008 in the United States, to overwhelming critical acclaim with some critics calling it the greatest comic-book based movie ever made. It also had enormous box office success, setting the record for the highest-grossing weekend opening in the U.S. with over $158 million and becoming the 3rd highest grossing film of all time domestically, and the sixth-highest worldwide at the time.

At the 2009 Golden Globe Awards, Christopher Nolan accepted the award for Best Supporting Actor in a Motion Picture on behalf of the deceased Heath Ledger. Nolan was nominated for the Directors Guild of America Award for Best Director for *The Dark Knight*. While the movie did not receive any nominations for the five major categories at the 81st Academy Awards, it was nominated for a total of eight Oscars, and won two, the Academy Award for Best Sound Editing, and a posthumous Academy Award for Best Supporting Actor for Ledger.

After the release of Nolan's successful 2008 film *The Dark Knight*, Warner Bros. contracted Nolan to a seven-figure deal to direct the science fiction film *Inception*. The film was based on a script written by Nolan and has been described as being "a contemporary sci-fi actioner set within the architecture of the mind". Filming began in summer 2009, and *Inception* was released on July 16, 2010 to largely positive reviews and became a box office hit.

Upcoming projects

On March 10, 2010, Nolan confirmed that he and David Goyer have been working on an idea for a Superman film. Nolan says, "He basically told me, 'I have this thought about how you would approach Superman.' I immediately got it, loved it and thought: That is a way of approaching the story I've never seen before that makes it incredibly exciting. I wanted to get Emma and I involved in shepherding the project right away and getting it to the studio and getting it going in an exciting way... A lot of people have approached Superman in a lot of different ways. I only know the way that has worked for us that's what I know how to do." It is unlikely that he will direct, but would have significant creative input in the process.

Nolan also confirmed his involvement with a sequel to *The Dark Knight* and gave some information regarding the story. The next Batman film will be Nolan's last in the series and a conclusion to the story. Nolan says, "Without getting into specifics, the key thing that makes the third film a great possibility for us is that we want to finish our story. And in viewing it as the finishing of a story rather than infinitely blowing up the balloon and expanding the story . . . I'm very excited about the end of the film, the conclusion, and what we've done with the characters. My brother has come up with some pretty exciting stuff." Warner Bros. has set the date for the next Batman film for July 20, 2012. On June 4, 2010 Christopher Nolan spoke with *Empire* magazine and confirmed that the Joker will not return. When asked for the reason he said, "No…I just don't feel comfortable about it."

Recurring collaborators

Nolan often casts certain actors more than once in his films. Christian Bale, Michael Caine, Cillian Murphy, Russ Fega and Larry Holden are among his most frequent acting collaborators.

Nolan's wife Emma Thomas has produced most of his films, with the exception of *Memento* and *Insomnia*. Lee Smith has been Nolan's editor since *Batman Begins*, with Dody Dorn editing *Memento* and *Insomnia*. Wally Pfister has served as cinematographer for all of Nolan's films starting with *Memento*. David Julyan has provided music for *Following*, *Memento*, *Insomnia*, and *The Prestige*. Hans Zimmer has provided music for *Batman Begins*, *The Dark Knight*, and *Inception*.

Actor	*Following* (1998)	*Memento* (2000)	*Insomnia* (2002)	*Batman Begins* (2005)	*The Prestige* (2006)	*The Dark Knight* (2008)	*Inception* (2010)
Christian Bale				✓	✓	✓	
Michael Caine				✓	✓	✓	✓
Russ Fega		✓			✓		✓
Morgan Freeman				✓		✓	
Larry Holden		✓	✓	✓			
Mark Boone Junior		✓		✓			
Nicky Katt			✓			✓	
Colin McFarlane				✓		✓	
Cillian Murphy				✓		✓	✓
John Nolan	✓			✓			
Gary Oldman				✓		✓	

Andrew Pleavin			✓			✓
Lucy Russell	✓		✓			
Jeremy Theobald	✓		✓			
Ken Watanabe			✓			✓

Filmography

Features

Year	Film	Studio	Worldwide Gross	Credit(s)
1998	*Following*	Momentum Pictures	$48,482 [3]	Director Writer Producer Cinematographer Editor
2000	*Memento*	Newmarket Films	$39,723,096 [4]	Director Writer
2002	*Insomnia*	Warner Bros.	$113,714,830 [5]	Director
2005	*Batman Begins*	Warner Bros.	$372,710,015 [6]	Director Writer
2006	*The Prestige*	Touchstone Pictures Warner Bros.	$109,676,311 [7]	Director Writer Producer
2008	*The Dark Knight*	Warner Bros.	$1,001,921,825 [8]	Director Writer Producer
2010	*Inception*	Warner Bros.	$804,305,974 [9]	Director Writer Producer

Short films

Year	Film	Credit(s)
1989	*Tarantella*	Director Writer Producer
1996	*Larceny*	Director Writer Producer
1997	*Doodlebug*	Director Writer Producer

Awards and nominations

Following (**1998**):

- Dinard British Film Festival: Silver Hitchcock (**won**)
- Dinard British Film Festival: Golden Hitchcock (*nominated*)
- Newport International Film Festival: Best Director Award (**won**)
- Newport International Film Festival: Jury Award - Best Film (*nominated*)
- Rotterdam International Film Festival: Tiger Award (**won**)
- Slamdance Film Festival: Black & White Award (**won**)
- Slamdance Film Festival: Grand Jury Prize (*nominated*)

Memento (**2000**):

- AFI Award: AFI Screenwriter of the Year (**won**)
- Academy Awards: Best Original Screenplay (with Jonathan Nolan, *nominated*)
- Critics Choice Award: Best Screenplay (**won**)
- DGA Award: Outstanding Directorial Achievement in Motion Pictures (*nominated*)
- Golden Globe: Best Screenplay (*nominated*)
- Independent Spirit Award: Best Director (**won**)
- Independent Spirit Award: Best Screenplay (**won**)
- MTV Movie Award: Best New Filmmaker (**won**)
- Satellite Award: Best Director (*nominated*)
- Satellite Award: Best Original Screenplay (*nominated*)
- Sundance Film Festival: Waldo Salt Screenwriting Award (with Jonathan Nolan, **won**)
- Sundance Film Festival: Grand Jury Prize - Dramatic (*nominated*)

Batman Begins (**2005**):

- Empire Awards: Best Director (*nominated*)
- Saturn Award: Best Writing (with David S. Goyer, **won**)

- Saturn Award: Best Director (*nominated*)

The Prestige (2006):

- Empire Awards: Best Director (**won**)

The Dark Knight (2008):

- Critics Choice Award: Best Director (*nominated*)
- DGA Award: Outstanding Directorial Achievement in Motion Pictures (*nominated*)
- Empire Awards: Best Director (**won**)
- PGA Award: Motion Picture Producer of the Year Award (*nominated*)
- Saturn Award: Best Writing (with Jonathan Nolan, **won**)
- Saturn Award: Best Director (*nominated*)
- WGA Award: Best Adapted Screenplay (with Jonathan Nolan and David S. Goyer, *nominated*)

Critical reception

Film	Rotten Tomatoes		Metacritic
	Overall	Top Critics	
Following	76%	N/A	N/A
Memento	93%	94%	80
Insomnia	92%	94%	78
Batman Begins	84%	60%	70
The Prestige	75%	57%	66
The Dark Knight	93%	91%	82
Inception	87%	79%	74
Average	**86%**	**79%**	**75**

See also

- Syncopy Films

Publications

Articles

- Charisma as Natural as Gravity [10], Christopher Nolan, *Newsweek*, 2008-01-26

External links

- NolanFans.com [11] Premiere Fan Community
- Christopher Nolan [12] at the Internet Movie Database
- Telegraph.co.uk [13] Interview with Christopher Nolan and Christian Bale

Personal Life

Emma Thomas

Emma Thomas	
 Thomas at WonderCon 2010.	
Born	Emma Thomas
Other names	Emma Thomas-Nolan
Occupation	Film producer
Years active	1997 - present
Spouse	Christopher Nolan

Emma Thomas is a film producer, known for co-producing husband Christopher Nolan's films.

Thomas worked as a script supervisor on many projects throughout the 1980s and 1990s, and was an assistant to director Stephen Frears on *High Fidelity*.

She lives with husband Nolan and their three children in Los Angeles, California.

Filmography

Producer

- *Doodlebug* (1997)
- *Following* (1998)
- *Memento* (2000) (associate producer)
- *Batman Begins* (2005)
- *The Prestige* (2006)
- *Batman: Gotham Knight* (2008)
- *The Dark Knight* (2008)
- *Inception* (2010)
- *The Man of Steel* (2012)
- *Untitled Batman Sequel* (2012)

See also

- Syncopy Films

External links

- Emma Thomas [1] at the Internet Movie Database
- Emma Thomas [2] at Allmovie

Jonathan Nolan

Jonathan Nolan	
Born	Jonathan Nolan 1976 London, United Kingdom
Occupation	Screenwriter
Citizenship	UK USA
Period	1998–present
Genres	crime, thriller
Relative(s)	Christopher Nolan (Brother)

Jonathan "Jonah" Nolan (born 1976) is a British-American author and screenwriter. His most famous work is the short story "Memento Mori", which was used by his brother, director Christopher Nolan, as the basis for the screenplay for the critically acclaimed film *Memento*. He has also co-written the screenplays for *The Prestige* and *The Dark Knight*, with his brother.

Early life

He was born in London, England, to an English father and American mother. He was raised in the Chicago area. Nolan attended Loyola Academy in Wilmette, Illinois, graduating in 1994, and then graduated from Georgetown University in Washington, D.C., in 1999, where he majored in English.

Works

Nolan describes his successful working relationship with his brother in the production notes of *The Prestige*: "I've always suspected that it has something to do with the fact that he's left-handed and I'm right-handed, because he's somehow able to look at my ideas and flip them around in a way that's just a little bit more twisted and interesting. It's great to be able to work with him like that." In addition, they also contrast in the way they speak: both brothers have a mixed dialect of American and English, but Jonathan in a more American accent and Christopher in a more English accent.

On March 23, 2007, it was announced he would pen *Interstellar*, a science fiction film. It is based on the theories of Kip Thorne, a theoretical physicist known for his prolific contributions in gravitation physics and astrophysics and for having trained a generation of scientists. The film is being directed by Steven Spielberg and is scheduled to be released in 2013.

At a Comic Con press conference on July 26, 2008, Nolan was confirmed by director McG to be the "lead writer" of *Terminator Salvation*, but was not listed under writing or story credits.

On February 9, 2010, it was revealed that Nolan is currently working with his brother and David S. Goyer on the third Batman film. It has also been reported that Nolan will be working on the next Superman film.

Filmography

- *Memento* (2000) - original story
- *The Prestige* (2006) - screenplay
- *The Dark Knight* (2008) - screenplay
- *Untitled Third Batman film* (2012) - screenplay
- *The Man of Steel* (2012) - screenplay
- *Interstellar* (2013) - screenplay

External links

- Jonathan Nolan [1] at the Internet Movie Database
- "Memento Man Revisits Hilltop" - article from *The Hoya* [2]

Genres of Films

Superhero film

A **superhero film**, **superhero movie**, or **superhero motion picture** is an action, fantasy or science fiction film that is focused on the actions of one or more superheroes, individuals who usually possess superhuman abilities relative to a normal person and are dedicated to protecting the public. These films are almost always action-oriented, and the first film of a particular character often includes a focus on the origin of the special powers including the first fight against the character's most famous archenemy or supervillain. The plot typically revolves around the efforts of the superheroes to thwart some dire peril of significant consequence.

Most superhero movies are adapted from comic books, where they are most prominent. Several such as *Darkman*, *The Meteor Man*, *Up, Up, and Away*, *The Incredibles* and *Hancock*, are original.

History

Early years

Almost immediately after superheroes rose to prominence in comic books, they were adapted into Saturday movie serials aimed at children, starting with *Adventures of Captain Marvel* (1941). Serials such as *Batman* (1943), *The Phantom* (1943), *Captain America* (1944), and *Superman* (1948) followed.

In the coming decades, the decline of Saturday serials and turmoil in the comic book industry put an end to superhero motion pictures, with the exception of episodes of the television series *Adventures of Superman*, starring George Reeves, which had been compiled for theatrical release, and *Batman* (1966) a big-screen extension of the *Batman* television series starring Adam West. Other superhero films released at this time include Mario Bava's *Danger: Diabolik* (1968) based on the Italian supervillain character Diabolik. Original superhero characters emerged in other more comedy oriented films such as the French political satire film *Mr. Freedom* (1969) and the American b-movies *Rat Pfink a Boo Boo* (1966) and *The Wild World of Batwoman* (1966).

Later years

Richard Donner's *Superman* (1978), the first major superhero feature film, proved a critical success and a commercial hit. The success of *Superman* wore into the 1980s, as more successful entries emerged throughout the decade, beginning with Richard Lester's *Superman II* (1980) and ending with Tim Burton's *Batman* (1989). Other films were released during the 1980s and 1990s including *Swamp Thing* (1982), *Superman III* (1983), *Supergirl* (1984), *The Toxic Avenger* (1985), *Superman IV: The Quest for Peace* (1987), *The Punisher* (1989), *Dick Tracy* (1990), *The Rocketeer* (1991), *Batman Returns* (1992), *The Shadow* (1994), *Batman Forever* (1995), *Mighty Morphin Power Rangers: The Movie* (1995), *The Phantom* (1996), and *Turbo: A Power Rangers Movie* (1997). Marvel Comics' *Captain America* (1991) didn't have a theatrical release and Roger Corman's *The Fantastic Four* (1994) was released neither theatrically nor on home video. Alex Proyas' *The Crow* (1994) became the first independent comics superhero film that established a franchise. As Joel Schumacher's *Batman & Robin* (1997) was critically panned for being too jokey and tongue-in-cheek, *The Crow* brought in a new realm of violence absent in previous popular superhero films targeted at younger audiences and bridging a gap to the more modern action film. The success of *The Crow* catalyzed the release of a film version of *Spawn* (1997), Image Comics' leading character. The success of the "darker" Image Comics characters shifted the direction of comic book movies. Marvel soon released their first film to become a franchise, *Blade* (1998). *Blade* was also a mix of a more traditional action film as well as darker superhero film with the title character having superpowers as well as carrying an assault of weaponry.

The 2000s

The 2000s brought forward some of the most profitable superhero franchises in history. It began with the surprise hit of Bryan Singer's *X-Men* (2000) which also became a film franchise but with less violence than the *Blade* series. Later, one of the largest blockbusters of all time was released with Sam Raimi's *Spider-Man* (2002). With high ticket and DVD sales, several new superhero films were released every year in the 2000s, including *Daredevil* (2003), *The League of Extraordinary Gentlemen* (2003), *Hulk* (2003), *Catwoman* (2004), *Hellboy* (2004), *The Punisher* (2004), *Batman Begins* (2005), *Fantastic Four* (2005), *Ghost Rider* (2007), *Iron Man* (2008), *Watchmen* (2009), *Kick Ass* (2010) and *Jonah Hex* (2010). Many sequels and spin-offs were also released throughout the decade, including *Blade II* (2002), *X2: X-Men United* (2003), *Spider-Man 2* (2004), *Blade: Trinity* (2004), *Elektra* (2005), *X-Men: The Last Stand* (2006), *Spider-Man 3* (2007), *Fantastic Four: Rise of the Silver Surfer* (2007), *Hellboy 2: The Golden Army* (2008), *The Dark Knight* (2008), *X-Men Origins: Wolverine* (2009), and *Iron Man 2* (2010). Non-Hollywood superhero films also were released including the American/Spanish production *Faust: Love of the Damned* (2001), Japan's *Ultraman* (2004), Bollywood's *Krrish* (2006) and Thailand's *Mercury Man* (2006). Several non-action film oriented superhero films were released in the 2000s with varying ranges of success.[citation needed] M. Night Shyamalan's *Unbreakable* (2000) is a thriller about a man who learns from a mysterious comic book dealer that he is destined to become a modern day superhero. Brad Bird's *The Incredibles* (2004) for Pixar was a critically acclaimed digitally-animated family oriented superhero film. Other hybrids include *Sky High* (2005) and "Zoom" (2006) which were fusions of the superhero and teen film genres, *My Super Ex-Girlfriend* (2006) a combination of superhero film and a romantic comedy.

Some series from the current and previous decades were also re-released, such as *Superman II: The Richard Donner Cut* (2006). Other series discarded the continuities of previously released films and began a reboot, most notably Christopher Nolan's *Batman Begins* (2005) as well as Louis Leterrier's *The Incredible Hulk* (2008) and Lexi Alexander's *Punisher: War Zone* (2008). Bryan Singer's *Superman Returns* (2006) is unique due to the fact that it is a sequel to the first two Superman films, yet also a reboot to the third and fourth films. Currently, the *Batman Begins* sequel *The Dark Knight* (2008) is not only the highest grossing comic book film of all time, it is also the most nominated superhero film in Academy Award history with 8 nominations including best supporting actor for Heath Ledger and also one of the highest grossing films of all time.

Upcoming projects as of August 2010

A *Superman Returns* sequel was planned for 2009 but delayed and later scrapped in favor of a reboot. Following references to the "Avenger initiative" in *Iron Man*, *Iron Man 2* and *The Incredible Hulk*, Marvel plans to release *Thor* on May 6, 2011. and *Captain America: The First Avenger* on July 22, 2011, leading up to the May 2012 release of *The Avengers*. *The Green Hornet* film is set for a January 14, 2011 release starring Seth Rogen. In 2008, there were reports that DC Comics planned to release *Green Arrow: Escape from Super Max*. A film about the character Venom is in development for an unknown date. Other intended releases include several *X-Men* spin-offs (The current one being called *X-Men: First Class*), *Silver Surfer*, *Ant-Man,* and movies regarding many DC superheroes such as Wonder Woman and the Flash. Warner Bros. has announced that a Green Lantern film will be released on June 17, 2011, to be directed by Martin Campbell and starring Ryan Reynolds as Hal Jordan, with a budget of $150 million. Despite initial reports of a forthcoming *Spider-Man 4* project filming was ultimately cancelled and, following new direction and different casting, plans for a reboot arose instantly. A Ghost Rider sequel titled *Ghost Rider: Spirit of Vengeance* is being planned to be released in February 17, 2012.

Parody

Kevin Smith's 2001 film *Jay and Silent Bob Strike Back*, parodies film companies' seemingly compulsive purchase of comic book film rights with "Bluntman and Chronic". In the film, the character Brodie Bruce describes the process: "After *X-Men* hit at the box office, the movie companies started buying out every comic property they could get their dirty little hands on". Mark Hamill's 2004 parody *Comic Book: The Movie*, about a comic book fan and a film adaptation of his favorite character, was released direct-to-video and achieved mild success,[*citation needed*] garnering a cult following among comic book readers. Craig Mazin directed the more direct parody *Superhero Movie*, released in 2008. Another comedic play on superheroes is The Specials, a film in which the title team is more concerned with their public image than actually being superheroes or saving people. This is filmed in an almost "mockumentary" style, and stars Jamie Kennedy, Rob Lowe, and Haden Church.

See also

- List of American superhero films
- List of films based on comics
- List of films based on DC Comics
- List of films based on Marvel Comics
- List of films based on Dark Horse Comics
- Fantasy film
- Action film
- Science fiction film
- Superhero live-action television series

Bibliography

- Lichtenfeld, Eric (2007). *Action Speaks Louder: Violence, Spectacle, and the American Action.* Wesleyan University Press. ISBN 0819568015.
- The Staff and Friends of Scarecrow (2003). *The Scarecrow Video Movie Guide.* Sasquatch Books. ISBN 1570614156.

External links

- ComicBookMovie.com [1]
- SuperheroHype.com [2]
- SuperheroesLives.com [3]
- SuperheroMovies.net [4]

Neo-noir

Neo-noir (from the Greek *neo,* new; and the French *noir,* black) is a style often seen in modern motion pictures and other forms that prominently utilize elements of *film noir,* but with updated themes, content, style, visual elements or media that were absent in *films noir* of the 1940s and 1950s.

History

Main article: film noir

The term *Film Noir* (French for "black film") was coined by critic Nino Frank in 1946, but was rarely used by film makers, critics or fans until several decades later. The classic era of *film noir* is usually dated to a period between the early 1940s and the late 1950s. Typically American crime dramas or psychological thrillers, *films noir* had a number of common themes and plot devices, and many distinctive visual elements. Characters were often conflicted antiheroes, trapped in a difficult situation and making choices out of desperation or nihilistic moral systems. Visual elements included low-key lighting, striking use of light and shadow, and unusual camera placement.

Although there have been few new major films in the classic *film noir* genre since the early 1960s, it has nonetheless had significant impact on other genres. These films usually incorporate both thematic and visual elements reminiscent of *film noir.* Both classic and neo-noir films are often independent features.

It wasn't until after 1970 that film critics began to consider "neo-noir" as a separate genre by its own definition. However, noir and post-noir terminology (such as "neo-classic," "hard-boiled", etc.) in modern application are often disclaimed by both critics and practitioners alike due to the obscurity of such an unrefined genre. For example, James M. Cain, author of *The Postman Always Rings Twice* and *Double Indemnity*, is considered to be one of the defining authors of hard-boiled fiction. Yet, Cain is quoted as saying, "I belong to no school, hard-boiled or otherwise, and I believe these so-called schools exist mainly in the imagination of critics, and have little correspondence in reality anywhere else."

Unlike classic *noirs,* neo-noir films are aware of modern circumstances and technology—details that were typically absent or unimportant to the plot of classic *film noir.* In the films of the early 1940s and '50s, audiences are led to understand and build a relationship with the protagonist or anti-hero. Neo-noir films of post-1970 often reverse this role. Unconventional camera movements and plot progression remind them that they are merely watching the film and not partaking in the story.

Modern themes employed in neo-noir films include identity crises, memory issues and subjectivity, and - most importantly - technological problems and their social ramifications. Because these fundamental elements are as ambiguous in practice as their definitions, film theorists argue that the term "neo-noir" can be applied to other works of fiction that similarly incorporate such motifs. Robert Arnett states that "Neo-noir has become so amorphous as a genre/movement, any film featuring a detective or crime qualifies." It is because of this genre's ambivalence that neo-noir is still shaped and interpreted so malleably today.

Others have noted that films like After Dark, My Sweet and Hard Eight are neo-noirs that seamlessly combine the noir genre with elements of the Western genre in terms of setting and themes.

See also

- List of film noir

References

Bibliography

- Arnett, R. (2006). Eighties noir: the dissenting voice in reagan's america. Journal of Popular Film & Television, 34(3)
- Conard, Mark T. *The Philosophy of Neo Noir.* University Press of Kentucky, 2006. (ISBN 0-81-312422-0)
- Hirsch, Foster *Detours and Lost Highways: A Map of Neo-Noir.* Proscenium Publishers Inc., New York, 1999. (ISBN 0-87910-288-8)
- Snee, B. J. (2009). Soft-boiled cinema: joel and ethan coens' neo-classical neo-noirs. Literature Film Quarterly, 37(3)
- Mark T. Conard: *The Philosophy of Neo-Noir.* University of Kentucky Press 2007, ISBN 9780813124223 (*restricted online copy* [1] at Google Books)

External links

- *An Introduction to Neo-Noir* [2] at Crime Culture by author Lee Horsley
- Neo-Noir Grosses [3] at Box Office Mojo

Thriller (genre)

Thriller is a genre of literature, film and television that uses suspense, tension and excitement as the main elements. The primary subgenres of thrillers are: mystery, crime and psychological thrillers. After the assassination of President Kennedy, political thriller and paranoid thriller films became very popular. The brightest examples of thrillers are the Hitchcock's movies.

Thrillers are mostly characterised by an atmosphere of menace, violence, crime and murder by showing society as dark, corrupt and dangerous, though they often feature a happy ending in which the villains are killed or arrested. Thrillers heavily promote on literary devices such as plot twists, red herrings and cliffhangers. They also promote on moods, such as a high level of anticipation, adrenaline rush, arousal, ultra-heightened expectation, uncertainty, anxiety and sometimes even terror. The tones in thrillers are usually gritty, slick and lurid.

The cover-up of important information from the viewer and fight/chase scenes are common methods in all of the thriller subgenres. Though each subgenre has its own characteristics and methods. Common methods in *crime thrillers* are mainly ransoms, captivities, heists, revenge, kidnappings and, more common in *mystery thrillers* are, investigations and the whodunit technique. Common elements in *psychological thrillers* are mind games, psychological themes, stalking, confinement/deathtraps, horror-of-personality and obsession. While elements such as conspiracy theories, false accusations, paranoia and sometimes action are common in *paranoid thrillers*.

"Homer's Odyssey is one of the oldest stories in the Western world and is regarded as an early prototype of the thriller." A thriller is villain-driven plot, whereby he presents obstacles that the hero must overcome.

Characteristics

A genuine, standalone thriller is a film that provide thrills and keeps the audience cliff-hanging at the 'edge of their seats' as the plot builds towards a climax. The tension usually arises when the character(s) is placed in a menacing situation, mystery, or an escape from which escaping seems impossible. Life is threatened, usually because the principal character is unsuspecting or unknowingly involved in a dangerous or potentially deadly situation.

Characters in thrillers include criminals, stalkers, assassins, innocent victims (often on the run), menaced women, characters with dark pasts, psychotic individuals, terrorists, cops and escaped cons, private eyes, people involved in twisted relationships, world-weary men and women, psycho-fiends, and more. The themes of thrillers frequently include terrorism, political conspiracy, pursuit, or romantic triangles leading to murder.

Thrillers mostly take place in ordinary suburbs/cities. Though sometimes, they may take place wholly or partly in exotic settings such as foreign cities, deserts, polar regions, or high seas. The heroes in most thrillers are frequently ordinary citizens unaccustomed to danger. However, more common in crime thrillers, they may also be "hard men" accustomed to danger, like, police officers and detectives. While such heroes have traditionally been men, women lead characters have become increasingly common.

Thrillers often overlap with mystery stories, but are distinguished by the structure of their plots. In a thriller, the hero must thwart the plans of an enemy, rather than uncover a crime that has already happened; while a murder mystery would be spoiled by a premature disclosure of the murderer's identity, in a thriller the identity of a murderer or other villain is typically known all along. Thrillers also occur on a much grander scale: the crimes that must be prevented are serial or mass murder, terrorism, assassination, or the overthrow of governments. Jeopardy and violent confrontations are standard plot elements. While a mystery climaxes when the mystery is solved, a thriller climaxes when the hero finally defeats the villain, saving his own life and often the lives of others. In thrillers influenced by film noir and tragedy, the compromised hero is often killed in the process.

In recent years, thrillers have been slightly influenced by the horror genre; they have more gore/sadistic violence, brutality, terror and body counts. Recent thrillers that did that are *Eden Lake*, *The Last House on the Left*, *P2*, *Untraceable* and *Funny Games*

Similar distinctions separate the thriller from other overlapping genres: adventure, spy, legal, war, maritime fiction, and so on. Thrillers are defined not by their subject matter but by their approach to it. Many thrillers involve spies and espionage, but not all spy stories are thrillers. The spy novels of John le Carré, for example, explicitly and intentionally reject the conventions of the thriller. Conversely, many thrillers cross over to genres that traditionally have had few or no thriller elements. Alistair MacLean, Hammond Innes, and Brian Callison are best known for their thrillers, but are also accomplished writers of man-against-nature sea stories.

Thrillers may be defined by the primary mood that they elicit: fearful excitement. In short, if it "thrills", it is a thriller. As the introduction to a major anthology explains,

> .[T]hrillers provide such a rich literary feast. There are all kinds. The legal thriller, spy thriller, action-adventure thriller, medical thriller, police thriller, romantic thriller, historical thriller, political thriller, religious thriller, high-tech thriller, military thriller. The list goes on and on, with new variations constantly being invented. In fact, this openness to expansion is one of the genre's most enduring characteristics. But what gives the variety of thrillers a common ground is the intensity of emotions they create, particularly those of apprehension and exhilaration, of excitement and breathlessness, all designed to generate that all-important thrill. By definition, if a thriller doesn't thrill, it's not doing its job.

—James Patterson, June 2006, "Introduction," Thriller

Writer Vladimir Nabokov, in his lectures at Cornell University, said that "In an Anglo-Saxon thriller, the villain is generally punished, and the strong silent man generally wins the weak babbling girl, but there is no governmental law in Western countries to ban a story that does not comply with a fond tradition, so that we always hope that the wicked but romantic fellow will escape scot-free and the good but dull chap will be finally snubbed by the moody heroine."

Sub-genres

See also: List of thriller films

The thriller genre can include the following sub-genres, which may include elements of other genres:

- **Conspiracy thriller**: In which the hero/heroine confronts a large, powerful group of enemies whose true extent only he/she recognizes. *The Chancellor Manuscript* and *The Aquitaine Progression* by Robert Ludlum fall into this category, as do films such as *Three Days of the Condor*, *Awake*, *Flightplan*, *Snake Eyes*, *Edge of Darkness*, *Absolute Power*, *Marathon Man*, *In The Line Of Fire*, *Capricorn One*, and *JFK*.

- **Crime thriller**: This particular genre is a hybrid type of both crime films and thrillers that offers a suspenseful account of a successful or failed crime or crimes. These films often focus on the criminal(s) rather than a policeman. Crime thrillers usually emphasise action over psychological aspects. Central topics of these films include serial killers/murders, robberies, chases, shootouts, heists and double-crosses. Some examples of crime thrillers involving murderers include, *Seven*, *A Perfect Murder*, *No Country for Old Men*, *Firewall*, *Hostage*, *Silence of the Lambs*, *Kiss the Girls* and *Copycat*. Examples of crime thrillers involving heists or robberies includes *The Asphalt Jungle*, *The Score*, *Rififi*, *Ocean's 11*, *Entrapment*, *The Killing* and *Reservoir Dogs*.

- **Disaster thriller**: In which the main conflict is due to some sort of natural or artificial disaster, such as floods, earthquakes, hurricanes, volcanoes, etc., or nuclear disasters as an artificial disaster. Examples include *Earthquake*, *2012*, *The Day After Tomorrow*, *Poseidon*, *Knowing*, *Deep Impact* and *Twister*.

- **Erotic thriller**: In which it consists of erotica and thriller. It has become popular since the 1980s and the rise of VCR market penetration. The genre includes such films as *Basic Instinct*, *Dressed to Kill*, *Color of Night*, *Eyes Wide Shut*, *Fatal Attraction*, *Looking for Mr. Goodbar*, *Obsessed*, and *In the Cut*.

- **Legal thriller**: In which the lawyer-heroes/heroines confront enemies outside, as well as inside, the courtroom and are in danger of losing not only their cases but their lives. *The Runaway Jury* by John Grisham is a well known example of the type. Other examples include *The Client*, *Fracture*, *A Time To Kill*, *Primal Fear*, *A Few Good Men*, *Presumed Innocent* and *The Juror*.

- **Medical thriller**: In which the hero/heroine are medical doctors/personnel working to solve an expanding medical problem. Robin Cook, Tess Gerritsen, Michael Crichton, and Gary Braver are well-known authors of this sub-genre. Nonfiction medical thrillers are also a subcategory, comprising works like *The Hot Zone* by Richard Preston. Films such as *Extreme Measures*, *The Experiment*, *Anatomy*, *Coma* and *Pathology* are other examples of medical thrillers.

- **Mystery thriller**: Suspense films where characters attempt solving, or involved in, a mystery. Examples include *Flightplan*, *Mindhunters*, *The Number 23*, *Unforgettable*, *Shutter Island*, *Secret Window*, *Vertigo*, *Identity* and *Memento*.

- **Political thriller**: In which the hero/heroine must ensure the stability of the government that employs him. The success of *Seven Days in May* (1962) by Fletcher Knebel, *The Day of the Jackal* (1971) by Frederick Forsyth, and *The Manchurian Candidate* (1959) by Richard Condon established this sub-genre. Examples include, *The Constant Gardner*, *Rendition*, *The Good Shepherd*, *Topaz*, *Syriana*, *The Interpreter* and *Proof of Life*.

- **Psychological thriller**: In which (until the often violent resolution) the conflict between the main characters is mental and emotional, rather than physical. The Alfred Hitchcock films *Suspicion*, *Shadow of a Doubt*, and *Strangers on a Train* and David Lynch's bizarre and influential *Blue Velvet* are notable examples of the type, as are *The Talented Mr. Ripley*, *House of 9*, *Phone Booth*, *Cape Fear*, *Red Eye*, *The River Wild*, *Psycho*, *P2*, *Breakdown*, *The Collector*, *Panic Room*, *Don't Say A Word*, *Frailty*, *The Good Son*, *Dead Calm*, *Funny Games* and *Misery*.

- **Rape and Revenge films**: Out of the sub-genres of exploitation film, this focuses more on the thriller elements such as suspense, tension, some action and fast-pacing rather than scares and the supernatural. Some famous rape and revenge films are The Last House on the Left, Irréversible, Thriller - A Cruel Picture, Baise-moi, Kill Bill and I Spit On Your Grave.

- **Religious thriller**: In which the plot is closely connected to religious objects, institutions and questions. While suspense stories have always shown a significant affinity for religion and philosophical issues (G.K. Chesterton's novel *The Man Who Was Thursday* has been called a "metaphysical thriller"; and Umberto Eco's novels *The Name of the Rose* and *Foucault's Pendulum* both display thriller characteristics), Dan Brown's 2003 best-seller *The Da Vinci Code* has led to a current boom in religiously oriented thrillers. Other examples include *the film version of The Da Vinci Code*, *The Devil's Advocate*, *The Ninth Gate*, *Angel Heart*, *The Sin Eater*, *The Omega Code* and *Angels & Demons*.

- **Supernatural thriller**: In which the film brings in an otherworldly element mixed with tension, suspense and plot twists. Sometimes the hero and/or villain has some psychic ability. Examples include, *Lady in the Water*, *Possession*, *Fallen*, *Frequency*, *In Dreams*, *Flatliners*, *Jacob's Ladder*, *The Skeleton Key*, *Signs*, *What Lies Beneath*, *Unbreakable*, *Rosemary's Baby*, *The Others*, *The Gift*, *The Dead Zone* and the TV series *Medium*.

- **Techno thriller**: A suspense film in which the manipulation of sophisticated technology plays a prominent part. Examples include *The Thirteenth Floor*; *The Matrix*; *Jurassic Park*; *I, Robot*; *Eagle Eye*; *Hackers*; *Futureworld*; *eXistenZ* and *Virtuosity*.

Although most thrillers are formed in some combination of the above, there are some however that are formed with other genres, which commonly are the horror genre, spy genre and the action/adventure genre.

Examples

Fiction and literature

See also: List of thriller writers

Ancient epic poems such as the *Epic of Gilgamesh*, Homer's *Odyssey* and the *Mahābhārata* use similar narrative techniques as modern thrillers. In the *Odyssey*, the hero Odysseus makes a perilous voyage home after the Trojan War, battling extraordinary hardships in order to be reunited with his wife Penelope. He has to contend with villains such as the Cyclops, a one-eyed giant, and the Sirens, whose sweet singing lures sailors to their doom. In most cases, Odysseus uses cunning instead of brute force to overcome his adversaries.

"The Three Apples", a tale in the *One Thousand and One Nights* (*Arabian Nights*), is the earliest known murder mystery and suspense thriller with multiple plot twists and detective fiction elements. In this tale, a fisherman discovers a heavy locked chest along the Tigris river and he sells it to the Abbasid Caliph, Harun al-Rashid, who then has the chest broken open only to find inside it the dead body of a young woman who was cut into pieces. Harun orders his vizier, Ja'far ibn Yahya, to solve the crime and find the murderer within three days. This whodunit mystery may be considered an archetype for detective fiction.

The Count of Monte Cristo is a swashbuckling revenge thriller about a man named Edmond Dantès who is betrayed by his friends and sent to languish in the notorious Château d'If. His only companion is an old man who teaches him everything from philosophy to mathematics to swordplay. Just before the old man dies, he reveals to Dantès the secret location of a great treasure. Shortly after, Dantès engineers a daring escape and uses the treasure to reinvent himself as the Count of Monte Cristo. Thirsting for vengeance, he sets out to punish those who destroyed his life.

The Thirty-Nine Steps is an early thriller by John Buchan, in which an innocent man becomes the prime suspect in a murder case and finds himself on the run from both the police and enemy spies.

Novelists closely associated with the genre include Eric Ambler, Sydney Bauer, Ted Bell, Dan Brown, Lincoln Child, Tom Clancy, Clive Cussler, Michael Crichton, Nelson DeMille, Ian Fleming, Ken Follett, Frederick Forsyth, Graham Greene, John Grisham, Robert Ludlum, Alistair MacLean, Andy McNab, David Morrell, James Phelan, Douglas Preston, and Matthew Reilly.

Notable contributors to the thriller genre

Writers

- Raymond Chandler
- Dashiell Hammett
- John le Carré
- Peter Benchley
- W.E.B. Griffin
- Perri O'Shaughnessy
- Robin Cook
- Eric Ambler
- Frederick Forsyth

- John Grisham
- Clive Cussler
- Joy Fielding
- Mark Berent
- William Bernhardt
- Richard North Patterson
- Michael Crichton
- Tom Clancy
- Mary Higgins Clark

- Mary Willis Walker
- John Lutz
- Michael Connelly
- Ian Fleming
- J.F. Freedman
- Scott Turow
- Eileen Dreyer
- Ken Follett

Directors

- Alfred Hitchcock
- Bryan Bertino
- John Boorman
- D.J. Caruso
- Henri-Georges Clouzot
- Joel and Ethan Coen
- Jonathan Demme
- Rebecca Grace Brown
- Brian De Palma
- David Fincher
- Gary Fleder
- James Foley
- John Frankenheimer
- William Friedkin
- Robert Harmon
- Mary Harron

- Jon Amiel
- Gregory Hoblit
- Stephen Hopkins
- John Huston
- Neil Jordan
- Philip Kaufman
- Stanley Kubrick
- Adrian Lyne
- John McTiernan
- Michael Mann
- Christopher Nolan
- Phillip Noyce
- Alan J. Pakula

- Wolfgang Petersen
- Roman Polanski
- Sydney Pollack
- Carol Reed
- Joel Schumacher
- Martin Scorsese
- Ridley Scott
- Tony Scott
- M. Night Shyamalan
- Steven Soderbergh
- Steven Spielberg
- Quentin Tarantino
- Tom Tykwer
- Paul Verhoeven
- Orson Welles

Television

There have been at least two television series called simply *Thriller*, one made in the U.S. in the 1960s and one made in the UK in the 1970s. Although in no way linked, both series consisted of one-off dramas, each utilising the familiar motifs of the genre.

24 is a fast-paced television series with a premise inspired by the War on Terror. Each season takes place over the course of twenty-four hours, with each episode happening in "real time". Featuring a split-screen technique and a ticking onscreen clock, *24* follows the exploits of federal agent Jack Bauer as he races to foil terrorist threats.

Lost, which deals with the survivors of a plane crash, sees the castaways on the island forced to deal with a monstrous being that appears as a cloud of black smoke, a conspiracy of "Others" who have kidnapped or killed their fellow castaways at various points, a shadowy past of the island itself that they are trying to understand, polar bears, and the fight against these and other elements as they struggle simply to stay alive and get out of the island.

Prison Break follows Michael Scofield, an engineer who has himself incarcerated in a maximum-security prison in order to break out his brother, who is on death row for a crime he did not commit. In the first season Michael must deal with the hazards of prison life, the other inmates and prison staff, and executing his elaborate escape plan, while outside the prison Michael's allies investigate the conspiracy that led to Lincoln being framed. In the second season, Michael, his brother and several other inmates escape the prison and must evade the nationwide manhunt for their re-capture, as well as those who want them dead.

Other examples include, Dexter, Criminal Minds, Without a Trace, CSI, The 4400, Numb3rs, The Twilight Zone and The X-Files.

See also

- Adventure novel
- International Thriller Writers
- Spy film
- Mystery film
- Horror film
- Action film
- Crime film

References

http://www.grindhousehorror.com

Famous Recurring Collaborators

Christian Bale

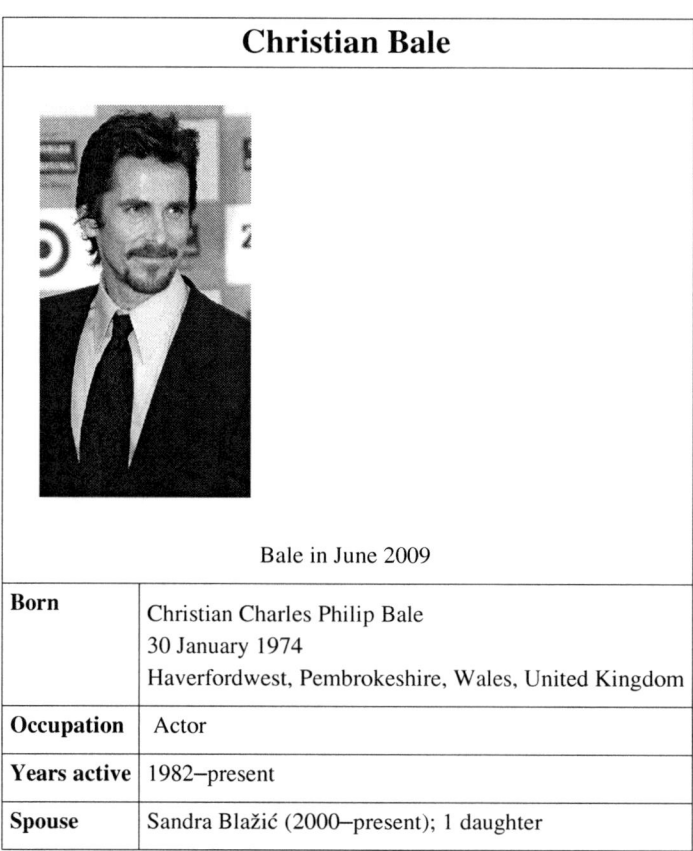

Christian Bale	
Born	Christian Charles Philip Bale 30 January 1974 Haverfordwest, Pembrokeshire, Wales, United Kingdom
Occupation	Actor
Years active	1982–present
Spouse	Sandra Blažić (2000–present); 1 daughter

Bale in June 2009

Christian Charles Philip Bale (born 30 January 1974) is an English actor. In addition to starring roles in big budget Hollywood films, he has long been heavily involved in films produced by independent producers and art houses.

Bale first caught the public eye when he was cast in the starring role of Steven Spielberg's *Empire of the Sun* at the age of 13, playing an English boy who is separated from his parents and subsequently finds himself lost in a Japanese internment camp during World War II. Since then, he has portrayed a wide range of characters. Bale is especially noted for his cult following: the tenth anniversary issue of *Entertainment Weekly* hailed him as one of the "Top 8 Most Powerful Cult Figures of the Past Decade", citing his cult status on the Internet. *EW* called Bale one of the "Most Creative People in

Entertainment" in anticipation of the release *American Psycho* (2000). *The Guardian* named Bale as one of the best actors never to have received an Academy Award nomination.

Early life

Bale was born in Wales to parents of English descent. His father, David Bale, was an entrepreneur, commercial pilot, and talent manager, and his mother, Jenny James, was a circus clown and performer. He is the youngest of four children. After leaving Britain in 1976, Bale spent his childhood in several countries, including Portugal and the United States.

Settling for four years in Bournemouth and Henley-on-Thames, Bale was educated at Shiplake Church of England Primary School; the independent Dolphin School, Berkshire; and at the Bournemouth School. He participated actively in rugby union. Bale has described his childhood, with respect to his mother being in the circus, as "interesting". He recalled his first kiss was with an acrobat named Barta.

As a child, he trained in ballet and guitar. His sister Louise's work in theatre also influenced his decision to become an actor. Bale's father was very supportive of his son's acting, resigning from his job as a commercial pilot to travel and manage Bale's burgeoning career. The elder Bale later married feminist icon Gloria Steinem, and died, aged 62, on 30 December 2003, from brain lymphoma.

Bale's first foray into acting was a commercial for the fabric softener Lenor in 1982, when he was eight years old. He appeared in a *Pac-Man* cereal commercial playing a child rock star a year later. In 1984 he made his stage debut in *The Nerd*, opposite Rowan Atkinson.

Career

1986–1998

Bale made his film debut as Tsarevich Alexei Nikolaevich of Russia in the made-for-television film *Anastasia: The Mystery of Anna* in 1986, which was followed by leading roles in the miniseries *Heart of the Country* and the fantasy adventure *Mio in the Land of Faraway*, in which he appeared for the first time with Christopher Lee and Nick Pickard.

A 14-year-old Bale in Stockholm, Sweden in February 1988 while promoting *Empire of the Sun*

In 1987, Amy Irving, his co-star in *Anastasia: The Mystery of Anna*, recommended Bale to her then-husband, Steven Spielberg, for a role in *Empire of the Sun*, adapted from the J.G. Ballard semi-autobiography. Bale's performance as Jim Graham earned him widespread critical praise and the first ever "Best Performance by a Juvenile Actor" award from the National Board of Review of Motion Pictures. The attention the press and his schoolmates lavished upon him after this took a toll on Bale, and he contemplated giving up acting until Kenneth Branagh approached him and persuaded him to appear in *Henry V* in 1989. In 1990 he played the role of Jim Hawkins opposite Charlton Heston (as Long John Silver) in *Treasure Island*, an adaptation of Robert Louis Stevenson's classic book.

In 1992, Bale starred as Jack Kelly in the Disney musical *Newsies*, and followed it up in 1993 with another release, *Swing Kids*, a movie about teenagers who secretly listened to forbidden jazz during the rise of Nazi Germany. Bale was recommended by actress Winona Ryder to star in Gillian Armstrong's 1994 film *Little Women*. Bale provided the voice for Thomas, a young compatriot of Captain John Smith, in Disney's *Pocahontas* (1995) and in 1997 played Arthur Stuart in *Velvet Goldmine*, Todd Haynes' tribute to glam rock. In 1999, Bale contributed to an all-star cast, including Kevin Kline, Michelle Pfeiffer, Stanley Tucci, and Rupert Everett, portraying Demetrius in an updated version of William Shakespeare's *A Midsummer Night's Dream*.

1999–2001

In 1999, Bale played serial killer Patrick Bateman in *American Psycho*, director Mary Harron's adaptation of Bret Easton Ellis' controversial novel. Bale was briefly dropped from the project in favor of Leonardo DiCaprio, but DiCaprio eventually dropped out to star in *The Beach*, and Bale was cast once again. He researched his character by studying the novel and prepared himself physically for the role by spending months tanning and exercising in order to achieve the "Olympian physique" of the character as described in the original novel. He went so far as to distance himself from the cast and crew to maintain the darker side of Bateman's character. *American Psycho* premiered at the 2000 Sundance Film Festival to much controversy. Roger Ebert condemned the film at first, calling it pornography and "the most loathed film at Sundance," but gave it a favourable review, writing that Harron "transformed a novel about bloodlust into a movie about men's vanity." Of Bale's performance, he wrote, "Christian Bale is heroic in the way he allows the character to leap joyfully into despicability; there is no instinct for self-preservation here, and that is one mark of a good actor."

On April 14, 2000, Lions Gate Films released *American Psycho* in theatres. Bale was later approached to make a cameo appearance in another Bret Easton Ellis adaptation, *The Rules of Attraction*, a film loosely connected to *American Psycho*, but he declined out of loyalty to Harron's vision of Bateman, which he felt could not be properly expressed by anyone else. In 2000, he again played a villain, this time in John Singleton's remake of the 1971 film, *Shaft*.

Bale has played an assortment of diverse characters since 2001. His first role after *American Psycho* was in the John Madden adaptation of the best-selling novel *Captain Corelli's Mandolin*. Bale played Mandras, a Greek fisherman who vied with Nicolas Cage's title character for the affections of the desirable Pelagia (Penelope Cruz). *Captain Corelli's Mandolin* was Bale's second time working with John Hurt, after *All the Little Animals*.

2002–2004

From 2002 to 2003, Bale starred in three feature films. *Laurel Canyon* (2002) was generally well received by critics. This film also marked the second time he worked with actress Kate Beckinsale, his costar in *Prince of Jutland* (1994). Critics generally focused on star Frances McDormand's performance over the rest of the cast.

Reign of Fire was Bale's first action vehicle and had, compared to all his previous work, an immense budget estimated at US$95,000,000. Bale entered into negotiations about starring in the film with reservations, but director Rob Bowman convinced him to take the lead role. Bale starred as Quinn Abercromby opposite Matthew McConaughey's Denton Van Zan. Bale and McConaughey trained for their respective roles by boxing and working out.

Equilibrium was Bale's third film of 2002, costing US$20 million to produce but earning just over US$5 million worldwide. In *Equilibrium*, Bale played John Preston, an elite law enforcer in a dystopian society. *Equilibrium* featured a fictional martial art called Gun Kata that combined gunfighting with hand-to-hand combat. According to moviebodycounts.com, the character of John Preston has the third most on-screen kills in a single movie ever with 118, exactly half of the movie's total of 236.

After a year's hiatus, Bale returned in 2004 to play Trevor Reznik, the title character in the psychological thriller *The Machinist*. Bale gained attention for his devotion to the role and for the lengths to which he went to achieve Reznik's emaciated, skeletal appearance. He went without proper rest for prolonged periods, and placed himself on a crash diet of generally coffee and apples, which reduced his weight by 63 pounds (4 st 4 lb/27 kg) in a matter of months. By the end of filming Bale weighed only 121 pounds (8 st 9 lb/55 kg), a transformation he described as "very calming mentally" and which drew comparisons to Robert De Niro's alternate weight-gaining regimen for his role as Jake LaMotta in the 1980 film *Raging Bull*. Bale claimed that he had not worked for a period of time before he was cast in the film. *"...I just hadn't found scripts that I'd really been interested in. So I was really dying for something to arrive. Then when this one did, I just didn't want to put it down. I finished it and, upon the kind of revelation that you get at the end, I immediately wanted to go back and re-visit it, to take a look at what clues I could have gotten throughout".* The Machinist was a low-budget production, costing roughly US$5 million to produce, and was given only a limited US release.

Bale, an admirer of Hayao Miyazaki's *Spirited Away*, was then cast as the voice of the title character, Howl, in the English language dub of the Japanese director's fantasy anime adventure *Howl's Moving Castle*, an adaptation of Diana Wynne Jones's children's novel. Its profits in the US were US$4,711,096, a fraction of its worldwide gross (US$235,184,110).

Batman: 2005–present

It was reported that Bale had previously auditioned for the role of Robin in *Batman Forever* (1995) and later *Batman and Robin* (1997), but lost out to Chris O'Donnell. However, this rumor was later dispelled by Bale himself in a magazine interview in 2008. In 2004, after completing filming for *The Machinist*, Bale won the coveted role of Batman and his alter ego Bruce Wayne in Christopher Nolan's *Batman Begins*, a reboot of the Batman film series. Bale beat out Jake Gyllenhaal, the closest competition for the role.

Still fresh off *The Machinist*, it became necessary for Bale to bulk up to match Batman's muscular physique. He was given a deadline of six months to do this. Bale recalled it as far from a simple accomplishment: "...when it actually came to building muscle, I was useless. I couldn't do one push up the first day. All of the muscles were gone, so I had a real tough time rebuilding all of that." With the help of a personal trainer, Bale succeeded in meeting the deadline, gaining a total of 100 lb (45 kg) in six months. He went from about 130 lbs to 230 lbs. He then discovered that he had actually gained more weight than the director desired, and dropped his weight to 190 lbs by the time filming began.

Bale had initial concerns about playing Batman, as he felt more ridiculous than intimidating in the Batsuit. He dealt with this by depicting Batman as a savage beast in his portrayal. To attain a deeper understanding of the character, Bale read various Batman comic books. He explained his interpretation of the young boy: "Batman is his hidden, demonic rage-filled side. The creature Batman creates is an absolutely sincere creature and one that he has to control but does so in a very haphazard way. He's capable of enacting violence — and to kill — so he's constantly having to rein himself in." For Bale, the most gruelling part about playing Batman was the suit. "You stick it on, you get hot, you sweat and you get a headache in the mask," he said. "But I'm not going to bitch about it because I get to play Batman." When promoting the film in interviews and public events, Bale retained an American accent to avoid confusion.

Batman Begins was released in the U.S. on June 15, 2005 and was a U.S. and international triumph for Warner Bros., costing approximately US$135 million to produce and taking in over US$370 million in returns worldwide. Bale earned the Best Hero award at the 2006 MTV Movie Awards for his performance.

Bale reprised his role as Batman in the *Batman Begins* sequel *The Dark Knight*. He trained in the Keysi Fighting Method, and performed many of his own stunts. *The Dark Knight* was released in the U.S. on July 18, 2008 and stormed through the box-office, with a record-breaking $158.4 million in the U.S. in its first weekend. It broke the $300 million barrier in 10 days, the $400 million mark in 16 days and the $500 million mark in 43 days, three new U.S. box office records set by the film. The film went on to gross over $1 billion at the box office worldwide, making it the fourth-highest grossing movie worldwide of all time, before adjusting for inflation.

It has been confirmed that Bale will star in the third projected movie in the rebooted franchise, that will be released on July 20, 2012, making Bale the actor who has played Batman more times than any other actor in feature film. Bale has given the same opinion as Nolan that, if the latter was forced to bring Robin into the films, he would never again play Batman; even though his favorite Batman story, *Batman: Dark Victory*, focuses on Robin's origin.

2006–2009

After *Batman Begins*, Bale returned to appearing in independent films. He was cast as one of the two leads in the South Central David Ayer-helmed crime drama *Harsh Times*, co-starring with Freddy Rodriguez and Eva Longoria. Bale played Jim Luther Davis, a grim Afghanistan War veteran afflicted with post-traumatic stress disorder, inexplicably approached by the Department of Homeland Security and hired as a federal agent. *Harsh Times* premiered at the 2005 Toronto International Film Festival and had a wide release on 10 November 2006.

Bale in 2008

Terrence Malick directed *The New World*, a period piece inspired by the stories of Pocahontas, and Bale was cast as John Rolfe. He shared the screen with Colin Farrell and Q'Orianka Kilcher, who played John Smith and Pocahontas. The majority of screen time was devoted to Farrell and Kilcher; Bale was a secondary character, and only appeared during the last third of the film. The film was a failure at the U.S. box office and its worldwide total (US$29,506,437) fell short of turning a profit (the production budget was placed at US$30 million).

In 2006, Bale took on four projects. *Rescue Dawn*, by German filmmaker Werner Herzog, had him playing U.S. Fighter pilot Dieter Dengler, who has to fight for his life after being shot down while on a mission during the Vietnam War. Bale left a strong impression on Herzog, with the director complimenting his acting abilities: "I find him one of the greatest talents of his generation. We made up our own minds long before he did *Batman*."

"I kind of like movies where I just get to just be dirty and crawling in the mud, "Rescue Dawn" it was all very primordial stuff, and with this one it was all about wearing the same clothes day after day and getting sweaty and dirty and sun exposure, and it's meant to be like that; Westerns are meant to be dirty, they shouldn't be all nice and clean. And I like getting my hand dirty."

Christian Bale on *3:10 to Yuma*

In *The Prestige*, an adaptation of the Christopher Priest novel about a rivalry between two Victorian stage magicians, Bale was reunited with *Batman Begins*' Michael Caine and director Christopher Nolan. The cast of *The Prestige* also included Hugh Jackman, Scarlett Johansson, Piper Perabo, and David Bowie. *I'm Not There*, a film in which Bale again worked alongside Todd Haynes and Heath Ledger (who would go on to play The Joker in *The Dark Knight*), is an artistic reflection of the life of Bob Dylan. He starred opposite Russell Crowe in a commercially and critically successful remake of the Western film *3:10 to Yuma*.

Bale was originally cast to play George W. Bush in Oliver Stone's film *W.*, but dropped out due to the prosthetics involved. Bale played John Connor in *Terminator Salvation* and FBI agent Melvin Purvis in Michael Mann's *Public Enemies*.

Writer/director Joe Carnahan confirmed in November 2007 that Bale is also involved in the upcoming movie *Killing Pablo* in which he is to play Major Steve Jacoby.

According to a *Nuts* magazine interview, Bale stated that he will be in the running to play the role of Solid Snake in a film adaptation of *Metal Gear Solid*. He has been cast alongside Mark Wahlberg in David O. Russell directed drama *The Fighter*.

Terminator Salvation incident

In July 2008, Bale had an angry tirade on the sets of *Terminator Salvation*, while filming in New Mexico. In February 2009, the audio recording of the incident was released. The tirade was directed at Shane Hurlbut, director of photography for the film. According to Bale, Hurlbut had, for the second time, ruined his concentration by walking into his line of sight during a scene. The recording is of a highly agitated Bale directing profanities at Hurlbut, threatening and belittling him, and finally threatening to quit the film if Hurlbut repeated his offence without being fired for it. It was reported that Warner film executives sent the tape to the insurer of the film in case Bale decided to quit the movie. In an interview with *E! Online*, assistant director and producer of *Terminator Salvation*, Bruce Franklin, said it was an isolated incident. *"If you are working in a very intense scene and someone takes you out of your groove ... It was the most emotional scene in the movie ... [A]nd for him to get stopped in the middle of it. He is very intensely involved in his character. He didn't walk around like that all day long. It was just a moment and it passed"*, Franklin said.

Actors Whoopi Goldberg and Terry Crews, directors Darren Aronofsky and Ron Howard, as well as *Ain't It Cool News* website creator Harry Knowles have also publicly defended Bale's actions, some of them citing the practice that crew members are to remain still while the camera is rolling. The incident also inspired experimental band The Mae Shi to write the song, "R U Professional", which features samples from the recording. Stephen Colbert parodied the incident on the 4 February 2009 episode of *The Colbert Report*, in which guest Steve Martin repeatedly walked in front of the camera and was berated by Colbert. The incident was re-enacted on *Late Night with Conan O'Brien*, with *Inside the Actor's Studio* host James Lipton giving performances of both Bale and the crewmember. An episode of the animated comedy series *Family Guy* also mixed in the voice of Peter Griffin interacting with Bale and reacting to Bale's comments as if they were directed at him to comedic effect.

After remaining silent for most of the week, Bale gave a public apology on 6 February 2009, to a Los Angeles radio station, KROQ. He stated that the outburst was "inexcusable" and that it was motivated by the day's shooting intensity. Bale said he "acted like a punk", and that he and Hurlbut talked after the incident and "resolved this completely". Bale acknowledged that the two worked together for several hours after the incident, and *"at least a month after that... I've seen a rough cut of the movie and he has done a wonderful job. It looks fantastic"*.

2010–present

In early 2010, Bale was confirmed to be starring in a romantic love story that will be directed by Terrence Malick and will also star Javier Bardem, Rachel McAdams and Olga Kurylenko.

Personal life

On 29 January 2000, Bale married Sandra "Sibi" Blažić (born 1970), a former model, make-up artist and personal assistant to Winona Ryder; the couple have a daughter, Emmeline, who was born on 27 March 2005 in Santa Monica, California. Since 1992, Bale has resided in Los Angeles.

Bale has three elder sisters – Erin Bale, a musician; Sharon Bale, a computer professional; and Louise Bale, a theatre actress and director. The Bale family is deeply rooted in show business, especially theatre. Bale is a distant relative of British actress Lillie Langtry, while his uncle, Rex Bale and maternal grandfather were actors as well.

Like his late father, businessman David (1941–2003), Christian Bale actively supports environmental groups such as Greenpeace and the World Wildlife Fund. Feminist activist Gloria Steinem became Christian Bale's stepmother when she married David Bale on 3 September 2000.; it was Steinem's first marriage (at the age of 66), and the couple were together until David Bale's death in 2003, aged 62.

During an interview promoting his 2009 film *Public Enemies* Bale said he is a video game fan, specifically of the *Metal Gear Solid* series. When questioned if he was in the running to play *Solid Snake*, Bale stated that he prefers to devote his spare time to constructive things and dislikes discussing his personal life.

Film and television credits

List of film and television credits

Year	Title	Role	Notes
1986	*Anastasia: The Mystery of Anna*	Alexei	television film
1987	*Heart of the Country*	Ben Harris	miniseries
1987	*Empire of the Sun*	Jamie "Jim" Graham	
1987	*Mio min Mio*	Benke Jum-Jum	
1989	*Henry V*	Falstaff's Boy	
1990	*Treasure Island*	Jim Hawkins	
1991	*A Murder of Quality*	Tim Perkins	television film
1992	*Newsies*	Jack "Cowboy" Kelly Francis Sullivan	
1993	*Swing Kids*	Thomas Berger	
1994	*Little Women*	Theodore "Laurie" Lawrence	
1994	*Prince of Jutland*	Amled	
1995	*Pocahontas*	Thomas	animated film voice only
1996	*The Portrait of a Lady*	Edward Rosier	
1996	*The Secret Agent*	Stevie	
1997	*Metroland*	Chris Lloyd	
1998	*Velvet Goldmine*	Arthur Stuart	
1999	*All the Little Animals*	Bobby Platt	
1999	*Mary, Mother of Jesus*	Jesus of Nazareth	television film
1999	*A Midsummer Night's Dream*	Demetrius	
2000	*Shaft*	Walter Wade, Jr.	
2000	*American Psycho*	Patrick Bateman	
2001	*Captain Corelli's Mandolin*	Mandras	
2002	*Equilibrium*	Cleric John Preston	
2002	*Reign of Fire*	Quinn Abercromby	
2002	*Laurel Canyon*	Sam Bentley	

2004	*Howl's Moving Castle*	Howl	English dub voice only
2004	*The Machinist*	Trevor Reznik	
2005	*Batman Begins*	Bruce Wayne/Batman	
2005	*The New World*	John Rolfe	
2006	*The Prestige*	Alfred Borden	
2006	*Harsh Times*	Jim Luther Davis	
2007	*Rescue Dawn*	Dieter Dengler	
2007	*I'm Not There*	Jack Rollins/Pastor John	
2007	*3:10 to Yuma*	Dan Evans	
2008	*The Dark Knight*	Bruce Wayne/Batman	
2009	*Terminator Salvation*	John Connor	
2009	*Public Enemies*	Melvin Purvis	
2010	*The Fighter*	Dick Eklund	*post-production*
2012	*Untitled Batman Project*	Bruce Wayne/Batman	*announced*

Awards and nominations

List of awards and award nominations

Year	Award	Award category	Title of work	Result
1987	NBR Award	Best Juvenile Performance	*Empire of the Sun*	Won
1989	Young Artist Awards	Best Young Actor in a Motion Picture–Drama	*Empire of the Sun*	Won
2001	Chlotrudis Awards	Best Actor	*American Psycho*	Won
2001	Empire Award	Best Actor	*American Psycho*	Nominated
2001	London Film Critics' Circle Awards	British Actor of the Year	*American Psycho*	Nominated
2001	OFCS Award	Best Actor	*American Psycho*	Nominated
2004	CIFF	Best Actor	*The Machinist*	Won
2005	Irish Film and Television Award	Best International Actor	*Batman Begins*	Nominated

2005	European Film Awards	Best Actor	*The Machinist*	Nominated
2005	Saturn Awards	Best Actor	*The Machinist*	Nominated
2006	London Film Critics' Circle Awards	British Actor of the Year	*The Machinist*	Nominated
2006	MTV Movie Awards	Best Hero	*Batman Begins*	Won
2006	Empire Awards	Best Actor	*Batman Begins*	Nominated
2006	Saturn Awards	Best Actor	*Batman Begins*	Won
2006	Scream Awards	Best Superhero	*Batman Begins*	Nominated
2006	Scream Awards	Most Heroic Performance	*Batman Begins*	Nominated
2007	Empire Award	Best Actor	*The Prestige*	Nominated
2007	San Diego Film Critics Society Awards	Special Award	*3:10 to Yuma, I'm Not There, Rescue Dawn*	Won
2007	Satellite Award	Best Actor in a Motion Picture, Drama	*Rescue Dawn*	Nominated
2008	London Film Critics' Circle Awards	British Actor of the Year	*3:10 to Yuma*	Nominated
2008	Independent Spirit Award	Robert Altman Award (with Todd Haynes, Laura Rosenthal, Cate Blanchett, Richard Gere, Heath Ledger, Ben Whishaw, Marcus Carl Franklin, Bruce Greenwood, Charlotte Gainsbourg)	*I'm Not There*	Won
2008	Scream Awards	Best Fantasy Actor	*The Dark Knight*	Nominated
2008	Scream Awards	Best Superhero	*The Dark Knight*	Won
2009	Empire Awards	Best Actor	*The Dark Knight*	Won
2009	People's Choice Awards	Favorite Male Action Star	*The Dark Knight*	Nominated
2009	People's Choice Awards	Favorite Leading Man	*The Dark Knight*	Nominated
2009	People's Choice Awards	Favorite Superhero	*The Dark Knight*	Won
2009	People's Choice Awards	Favorite On Screen Match Up (with Heath Ledger)	*The Dark Knight*	Won
2009	People's Choice Awards	Favorite Cast (with Heath Ledger, Gary Oldman, Michael Caine, Morgan Freeman, Aaron Eckhart, Maggie Gyllenhaal)	*The Dark Knight*	Won
2009	West Point Cadet Choice Awards	Best Exemplification of Leadership		Won

External links

- Christian Bale [1] at the Internet Movie Database
- Christian Bale [2] at Allmovie
- Christian Bale [3] at Yahoo! Movies
- Christian Bale [4] at TV.com
- Christian Bale [5] at the Open Directory Project

Morgan Freeman

Morgan Freeman	
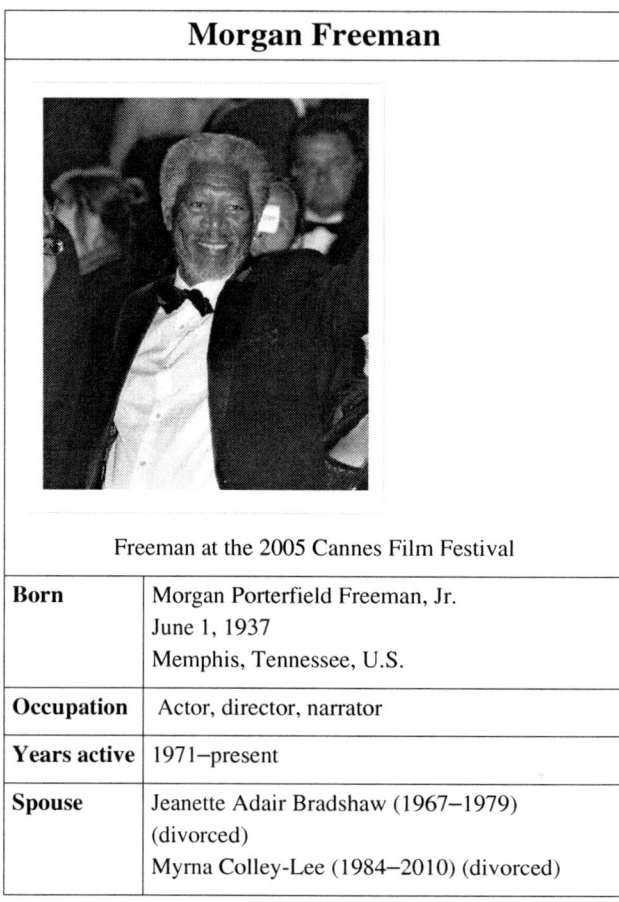 Freeman at the 2005 Cannes Film Festival	
Born	Morgan Porterfield Freeman, Jr. June 1, 1937 Memphis, Tennessee, U.S.
Occupation	Actor, director, narrator
Years active	1971–present
Spouse	Jeanette Adair Bradshaw (1967–1979) (divorced) Myrna Colley-Lee (1984–2010) (divorced)

Morgan Porterfield Freeman, Jr. (born June 1, 1937) is an American actor, film director, and narrator. He is noted for his reserved demeanor and authoritative speaking voice.

Freeman has received Academy Award nominations for his performances in *Street Smart*, *Driving Miss Daisy*, *The Shawshank Redemption* and *Invictus* and won in 2005 for *Million Dollar Baby*. He has also won a Golden Globe Award and a Screen Actors Guild Award.

Freeman has appeared in many other box office hits, including *Unforgiven*, *Glory*, *Seven*, *Deep Impact*, *The Sum of All Fears*, *Bruce Almighty*, *Batman Begins*, *The Bucket List*, *Evan Almighty*, *Wanted*, and *The Dark Knight*.

Early life

Morgan Freeman was born in Memphis, Tennessee, the son of Mayme Edna (née Revere) and Morgan Porterfield Freeman, Sr., a barber who died in 1961 from cirrhosis. He has three older siblings. Freeman was sent as an infant to his paternal grandmother in Charleston, Mississippi. His family moved frequently during his childhood, living in Greenwood, Mississippi; Gary, Indiana; and finally Chicago, Illinois. Freeman made his acting debut at age 9, playing the lead role in a school play. He then attended Broad Street High School, currently Threadgill Elementary School, in Mississippi. At age 12, he won a statewide drama competition, and while still at Broad Street High School, he performed in a radio show based in Nashville, Tennessee. In 1955, he graduated from Broad Street High School, but turned down a partial drama scholarship from Jackson State University, opting instead to work as a mechanic in the United States Air Force.

Freeman moved to Los Angeles in the early 1960s and worked as a transcript clerk at Los Angeles Community College. During this period, he also lived in New York City, working as a dancer at the 1964 World's Fair, and in San Francisco, where he was a member of the Opera Ring music group. Freeman acted in a touring company version of *The Royal Hunt of the Sun,* and also appeared as an extra in the 1965 film *The Pawnbroker.* He made his off-Broadway debut in 1967, opposite Viveca Lindfors in *The Nigger Lovers* (about the civil rights era "Freedom Riders"), before debuting on Broadway in 1968's all-black version of *Hello, Dolly!,* which also starred Pearl Bailey and Cab Calloway.

Career

Although his first credited film appearance was in 1971's *Who Says I Can't Ride a Rainbow?*, Freeman first became known in the American media through roles on the soap opera *Another World* and the PBS kids' show *The Electric Company*, (notably as Easy Reader and Vincent the Vegetable Vampire) which he later said he should have left earlier than he did.

Beginning in the mid-1980s, Freeman began playing prominent supporting roles in many feature films, earning him a reputation for depicting wise, fatherly characters. As he

Freeman at the *10 Items or Less* premiere in Madrid with co-star Paz Vega.

gained fame, he went on to bigger roles in films such as the chauffeur Hoke in *Driving Miss Daisy*, and Sergeant Major Rawlins in *Glory* (both in 1989). In 1994 he portrayed Red, the redeemed convict in the acclaimed *The Shawshank Redemption.* He also starred in films such as *Robin Hood: Prince of Thieves*, *Unforgiven*, *Seven*, and *Deep Impact.* In 1997, Freeman, together with Lori McCreary, founded the movie production company Revelations Entertainment, and the two co-head its sister online movie distribution company ClickStar. Freeman also hosts the channel *Our Space* on ClickStar, with specially crafted film clips in which he shares his love for the sciences, especially space exploration and aeronautics.

After three previous nominations—a supporting actor nomination for *Street Smart*, and leading actor nominations for *Driving Miss Daisy*, and *The Shawshank Redemption*—he won the Academy Award for Best Supporting Actor for his performance in *Million Dollar Baby* at the 77th Academy Awards. Freeman is recognized for his distinctive voice, making him a frequent choice for narration. In 2005 alone, he provided narration for two films, *War of the Worlds* and the Academy Award-winning documentary film *March of the Penguins*.

Freeman appeared as God in the hit movie *Bruce Almighty* and its sequel, *Evan Almighty*, as well as Lucius Fox in the critical and commercial success *Batman Begins* and its 2008 sequel, *The Dark Knight*. He starred in Rob Reiner's 2007 film *The Bucket List*, opposite Jack Nicholson. He teamed with Christopher Walken and William H. Macy for the comedy *The Maiden Heist*, which was released direct to video due to financial problems of the distribution company. In 2008, Freeman returned to Broadway to co-star with Frances McDormand and Peter Gallagher for a limited engagement of Clifford Odets's play, *The Country Girl*, directed by Mike Nichols.

He had wanted to do a film based on Nelson Mandela for some time. At first he tried to get Mandela's autobiography, *Long Walk to Freedom*, adapted into a finished script, but it could never be finalized. In 2007 he purchased the film rights to a pre-published 2008 book by John Carlin, *Playing the Enemy: Nelson Mandela and the Game that Made a Nation*. Clint Eastwood directed the Nelson Mandela bio-pic titled *Invictus*, starring Freeman as Mandela and Matt Damon as rugby team captain Francois Pienaar. It was reported in July 2009 that Freeman is in talks to co-star alongside Bruce Willis in *Red*.

Effective January 4, 2010, Freeman replaced Walter Cronkite as the voiceover introduction to the *CBS Evening News* featuring Katie Couric as news anchor. CBS cited the need for consistency in introductions for regular news broadcasts and special reports as the basis for the change.

As of 2010, Freeman is the host and narrator of the Discovery Channel television show *Through the Wormhole*.

Personal life

Family

Freeman was married to Jeanette Adair Bradshaw from October 22, 1967, until 1979. He married Myrna Colley-Lee on June 16, 1984. The couple separated in December 2007. Freeman's attorney and business partner, Bill Luckett, announced in August 2008 that Freeman and his wife are in the process of divorce. On 15 September 2010, their divorce was finalized in Mississippi.

Freeman and his wife, Myrna Colley-Lee, at the 1990 Academy Awards

He has two sons from previous relationships before he married Bradshaw. He adopted his first wife's daughter and the couple also had his fourth child.

Properties

Freeman lives in Charleston, Mississippi, and New York City. He co-owns and operates Madidi, a fine dining restaurant, and Ground Zero, a blues club, both located in Clarksdale, Mississippi. He officially opened his second Ground Zero in Memphis, Tennessee on April 24, 2008.

Criticism

Freeman has publicly criticized the celebration of Black History Month and does not participate in any related events, saying, "I don't want a black history month. Black history is American history." He says the only way to end racism is to stop talking about it, and he notes that there is no "white history month". Freeman once said on an interview with *60 Minutes*' Mike Wallace: "I am going to stop calling you a white man and I'm going to ask you to stop calling me a black man." Freeman supported the defeated proposal to change the Mississippi state flag, which contains the Confederate battle flag.

Honors

On October 28, 2006, Freeman was honored at the first Mississippi's Best Awards in Jackson, Mississippi, with the Lifetime Achievement Award for his works on and off the big screen. He received an honorary degree of Doctor of Arts and Letters from Delta State University during the school's commencement exercises on May 13, 2006.

In 2008 Freeman's family history was profiled on the PBS series *African American Lives 2*. A DNA test showed that he is descended from the Songhai and Tuareg peoples of Niger.

Charitable Work

In 2004 Freeman and others formed the Grenada Relief Fund to aid people affected by Hurricane Ivan on the island of Grenada. The Grenada Relief Fund has since become PLANIT NOW, an organization that seeks to provide preparedness resources for people living in hurricane and severe-storm afflicted areas.

Freeman has worked on narrating small clips for global organizations, such as One Earth, whose goals include raising awareness of environmental issues. He has narrated the clip "Why Are We Here", which can be viewed on One Earth's website.

Freeman has donated money to the Mississippi Horse Park in Starkville, Mississippi. The Horse park is part of Mississippi State University. Freeman has several horses that he takes there.

Politics

Freeman endorsed Barack Obama's candidacy for the United States presidential election, 2008, although he stated that he would not join Obama's campaign. He narrates for The Hall of Presidents with Barack Obama, who has been added to the exhibit. The Hall of Presidents re-opened on July 4, 2009 at Walt Disney World Resort in Orlando, Florida.

Car Accident

Freeman was injured in an automobile accident near Ruleville, Mississippi, on the night of August 3, 2008. The vehicle in which he was traveling, a 1997 Nissan Maxima, left the highway and flipped over several times. He and a female passenger, Demaris Meyer, were rescued from the vehicle using the "Jaws of Life". Freeman was taken via medical helicopter to The Regional Medical Center (The Med) hospital in Memphis. Police ruled out alcohol as a factor in the crash. Freeman was coherent following the crash, as he joked to a photographer about taking his picture at the scene. He broke his shoulder, arm and elbow in the crash and had surgery on August 5, 2008. Doctors operated for four hours to repair nerve damage in his shoulder and arm. His publicist announced he was expected to make a full recovery. Meyer, his passenger, has sued him for negligence, claiming that he was drinking the night of the accident. She has denied reports that they were romantically involved.

Miscellaneous

In July 2009 Freeman was one of the presenters at the 46664 concert (celebrating Nelson Mandela's birthday) at Radio City Music Hall in New York City.

Freeman was the first American to record a par on Legend Golf & Safari Resort's Extreme 19th hole.

Freeman has a private pilot's license, which he earned at age 65.

Filmography

Films

Year	Film	Role	Notes
1980	*Brubaker*	Walter	
1981	*Eyewitness*	Lieutenant Black	
1984	*Teachers*	Al Lewis	
	Harry & Son	Siemanowski	
1985	*Marie*	Charles Traughber	
	That Was Then... This Is Now	Charlie Woods	
1987	*Street Smart*	Fast Black	Independent Spirit Award for Best Supporting Male Nominated — Academy Award for Best Supporting Actor Nominated — Golden Globe Award for Best Supporting Actor - Motion Picture
1988	*Clean and Sober*	Craig	
1989	*Glory*	Sgt. Maj. John Rawlins	
	Driving Miss Daisy	Hoke Colburn	Golden Globe Award for Best Actor - Motion Picture Musical or Comedy National Board of Review Award for Best Actor Nominated — Academy Award for Best Actor
	Lean on Me	Principal Joe Clark	
	Johnny Handsome	Lt. A.Z. Drones	

1990	*The Bonfire of the Vanities*	Judge Leonard White	
	The Civil War	Voice of Frederick Douglass	
1991	*Robin Hood: Prince of Thieves*	Azeem	Nominated — MTV Movie Award for Best On-Screen Duo shared with Kevin Costner
1992	*Unforgiven*	Ned Logan	
	The Power of One	Geel Piet	
1993	*Bopha!*		director only
1994	*The Shawshank Redemption*	Ellis Boyd "Red" Redding, Narrator	Nominated — Academy Award for Best Actor Nominated — Golden Globe Award for Best Actor - Motion Picture Drama Nominated — Screen Actors Guild Award for Outstanding Performance by a Male Actor in a Leading Role - Motion Picture
1995	*Outbreak*	Brig. Gen. Billy Ford	
	Se7en	Detective Lt. William Somerset	Nominated — MTV Movie Award for Best On-Screen Duo shared with Brad Pitt Nominated — Saturn Award for Best Actor
1996	*Chain Reaction*	Paul Shannon	
	Moll Flanders	Hibble	
	Cosmic Voyage	Narrator	
1997	*Amistad*	Theodore Joadson	
	Kiss The Girls	Dr. Alex Cross	
	The Long Way Home	Narrator	
1998	*Deep Impact*	President Tom Beck	
	Hard Rain	Jim	
2000	*Nurse Betty*	Charlie Quinn	
	Under Suspicion	Victor Benezet	
2001	*Along Came a Spider*	Dr. Alex Cross	
2002	*The Sum of All Fears*	DCI William Cabot	
	High Crimes	Charlie Grimes	

2003	*Bruce Almighty*	God	
	Dreamcatcher	Col. Abraham Curtis	
	Levity	Pastor Miles Evans	
	Drug War	Lt. Redding	
2004	*Million Dollar Baby*	Eddie "Scrap Iron" Dupris	Academy Award for Best Supporting Actor Screen Actors Guild Award for Outstanding Performance by a Male Actor in a Supporting Role - Motion Picture Nominated — Golden Globe Award for Best Supporting Actor - Motion Picture Nominated — Screen Actors Guild Award for Outstanding Performance by a Cast in a Motion Picture
	The Hunting of the President	Narrator	limited release
	The Big Bounce	Walter Crewes	
2005	*An Unfinished Life*	Mitch Bradley	
	War of the Worlds	Narrator	
	March of the Penguins	Narrator	
	Batman Begins	Lucius Fox	
	Unleashed	Sam	
2006	*Edison Force*	Ashford	
	The Contract	Frank Carden	
	Lucky Number Slevin	The Boss	
	10 Items or Less	Himself	
2007	*Evan Almighty*	God	
	Feast of Love	Harry Stephenson	
	Gone, Baby, Gone	Jack Doyle	
	The Bucket List	Carter Chambers	Also Narrator
2008	*Wanted*	Sloan	
	The Love Guru	Narrator	Voice
	The Dark Knight	Lucius Fox	

2009	Prom Night in Mississippi	Himself	limited release
	Thick as Thieves	Keith Ripley	
	The Maiden Heist	Charlie	
	Invictus	Nelson Mandela	NAACP Image Award for Outstanding Actor in a Motion Picture National Board of Review Award for Best Actor tied with George Clooney for *Up in the Air* Nominated — Academy Award for Best Actor Nominated — Broadcast Film Critics Association Award for Best Actor Nominated — Golden Globe Award for Best Actor – Motion Picture Drama Nominated — Houston Film Critics Society Award for Best Actor Nominated — Screen Actors Guild Award for Outstanding Performance by a Male Actor in a Leading Role Nominated — Washington D.C. Area Film Critics Association for Best Actor
2010	Red	Joe	filming
2011	Dolphin Tale	Dr. McCarthy	pre-production

Television appearances

Year	Title	Role	Notes
1971–1977	The Electric Company	Easy Reader, DJ Mel Mounds, Dracula, Vincent the Vegetable Vampire	television series
1978	Roll of Thunder, Hear My Cry	Uncle Hammer	made-for-television
1981	The Marva Collins Story	Clarence Collins	made-for-television
1985	The Twilight Zone	Tony	Television series (episode "Dealer's Choice")
1986	Resting Place	Luther Johnson	made-for-television
1987	Fight For Life	Dr. Sherard	made-for-television

2008	*Smithsonian Channel's Sound Revolution*	Himself (host)	television series, series host
	Stephen Fry in America	Himself	television series, appears in episode 3
2010	*The Colbert Report*	Himself	interview
	The Daily Show	Himself	interview
	Through the Wormhole with Morgan Freeman	Himself (host)	television series, series host
	Saturday Night Live	Himself (celebrity cameo)	What Up With That

Other awards and honors

- 1978 Nominated for Tony Award for Best Performance by a Featured Actor in a Play in *The Mighty Gents*
- 1997 Received an honorary degree from Rhodes College, becoming an honorary alumnus
- 2003 Received the Crystal Globe award for outstanding artistic contribution to world cinema at the Karlovy Vary International Film Festival
- 2006 Guest of honor at the Cairo International Film Festival
- 2007 He and his wife received the Lifetime Achievement Award from the Mississippi Institute of Arts and Letters
- 2007 Outstanding Contribution To Film And TV gong at the Screen Nation Film and TV Awards
- 2008 Kennedy Center Honors
- 2010 Received an honorary degree from Brown University

External links

- Morgan Freeman [1] at the Internet Movie Database
- Morgan Freeman [2] at the Internet Broadway Database
- Morgan Freeman [3] at the Internet Off-Broadway Database
- Morgan Freeman [4] at Allmovie
- ClickStar [5] headed by Morgan Freeman and Lori McCreary
- Revelations Entertainment [6] Production company co-founded by Freeman
- A detailed biography of his history as an actor [7]
- Morgan Freeman movies at Movie Information [8]

1. REDIRECT Template:Navboxes

Michael Caine

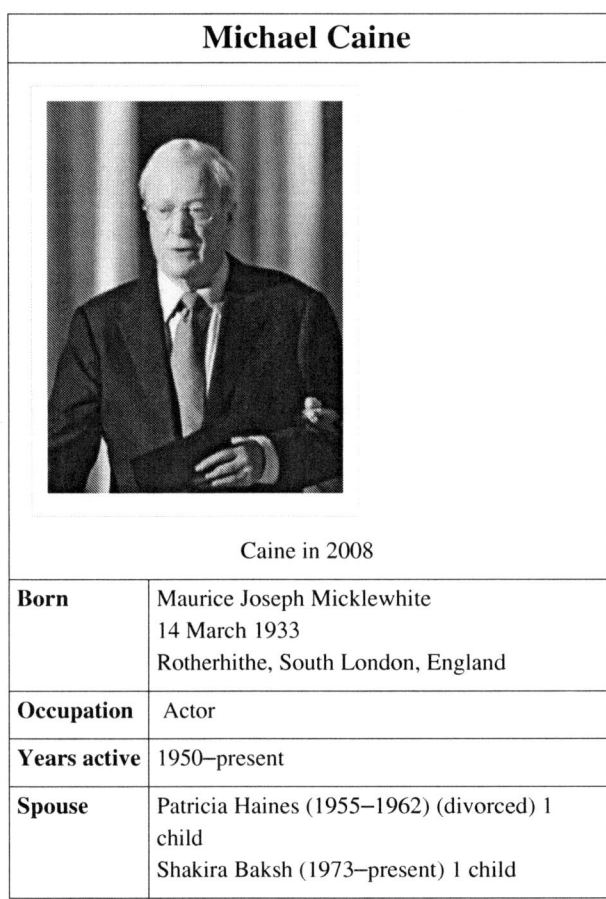

Michael Caine

Caine in 2008

Born	Maurice Joseph Micklewhite 14 March 1933 Rotherhithe, South London, England
Occupation	Actor
Years active	1950–present
Spouse	Patricia Haines (1955–1962) (divorced) 1 child Shakira Baksh (1973–present) 1 child

Sir Michael Caine, CBE (born **Maurice Joseph Micklewhite**; 14 March 1933) is an English film actor. Caine has appeared in over one hundred films.

He became well known for a number of popular and notable critically acclaimed performances, particularly in films such as *Zulu* (1964); *The Ipcress File* (1965); *Alfie* (1966); *The Italian Job* (1969); *The Battle Of Britain* (1969); *Get Carter* (1971); *The Man Who Would Be King* (1975); *Educating Rita* (1983); *Without a Clue* (1988); *Dirty Rotten Scoundrels* (1988); *The Muppet Christmas Carol* (1992); *Secondhand Lions* (2003); Academy Award–winning performances for best supporting actor in both *Hannah and Her Sisters* (1986), and *The Cider House Rules* (1999); as Nigel Powers in the parody *Austin Powers in Goldmember* (2002); and more recently as Alfred Pennyworth, the butler from *Batman Begins* (2005), and *The Dark Knight* (2008), and the protagonist in *Harry Brown* (2009). Most recently, he appeared as Miles, a supporting character in the film *Inception* (2010).

Caine is one of only two actors nominated for an Academy Award for acting (either lead or supporting) in every decade from the 1960s to 2000s (the other one being Jack Nicholson). In 2000, Caine was knighted by Queen Elizabeth II, in recognition of his contribution to cinema.

Early life

Caine was born **Maurice Joseph Micklewhite** in Rotherhithe, South East London, the son of Ellen Frances Marie (née Burchell), a cook and charlady, and Maurice Joseph Micklewhite, a fish market porter. His father was of part Romani (Gypsy) ancestry and a Catholic, though Caine was brought up in his Protestant mother's religion.

Caine grew up in Camberwell, London, and during the Second World War he was evacuated to North Runcton, in Norfolk. In 1944, he passed his eleven plus exam, winning a scholarship to Hackney Downs Grocers School. After a year there he moved to Wilson's Grammar School in Camberwell (now Wilson's School in Wallington South London), which he left at sixteen after gaining a School Certificate in six subjects. He then worked briefly as a filing clerk and messenger for a film company in Victoria Street and the film producer Jay Lewis in Wardour Street. From 1952, when he was called up to do his National Service, until 1954, he served in the British Army's Royal Fusiliers, first at the BAOR HQ in Iserlohn, Germany and then on active service during the Korean War. Caine has said he would like to see the return of National Service to help combat youth violence, stating: "I'm just saying, put them in the Army for six months. You're there to learn how to defend your country. You belong to the country. Then when you come out, you have a sense of belonging rather than a sense of violence."

Career

When Micklewhite first became an actor, he adopted the stage name "Michael Scott". His agent soon informed him, however, that another actor was already using the same name, and that he had to come up with a new name immediately. Speaking to his agent from a telephone box in Leicester Square, London, he looked around for inspiration, noted that *The Caine Mutiny* was being shown at the Odeon Cinema, and decided to change his name to "Michael Caine". He has joked in interviews that had he looked the other way, he would have ended up as "Michael One Hundred and One Dalmatians".

1960s

Caine's acting career began in Horsham, Sussex. He responded to an advertisement for an assistant stage manager for the Horsham-based Westminster Repertory Company. This led to walk-on roles at the Carfax Theatre. After dozens of minor TV roles, Caine entered the public eye as the upper class British Army officer Gonville Bromhead VC in the 1964 film *Zulu*. This proved paradoxical, as Caine was to become notable for using a regional accent, rather than the Received Pronunciation hitherto considered proper for film actors. At the time, Caine's working class Cockney, just as with The Beatles'

Liverpudlian accents, stood out to American and British audiences alike. *Zulu* was closely followed by two of his best-known roles: the spy Harry Palmer in *The Ipcress File* (1965), and the womanising title character in *Alfie* (1966). He went on to play Palmer in a further four films, *Funeral in Berlin* (1966), *Billion Dollar Brain* (1967), *Bullet to Beijing* (1995) and *Midnight in Saint Petersburg* (1995). Caine made his first film in the United States in 1966, after an invitation from Shirley MacLaine to play opposite her in *Gambit*. During the first two weeks, whilst staying at The Beverly Hills Hotel, he met long term friends John Wayne and agent "Swifty" Lazar.

1970s

After working on *The Italian Job*, with Noël Coward, and a solid role as an RAF fighter pilot, Squadron Leader Canfield, in the all-star cast of *Battle of Britain* (both 1969), Caine played the lead in *Get Carter* (1971), a British gangster film. Caine was busy with successes including *Sleuth* (1972), opposite Laurence Olivier and *The Man Who Would Be King* (1975), co-starring Sean Connery and directed by John Huston (which he has stated will be the film he wishes to be remembered for after his death). In 1976, he appeared in the screen adaptation by Tom Mankiewicz of the Jack Higgins novel, *The Eagle Has Landed*, as *Oberst* (Colonel) Kurt Steiner, the commander of a Luftwaffe paratroop brigade disguised as Polish paratroopers, whose mission was to kidnap or kill the then-British Prime Minister, Winston Churchill, alongside co-stars Donald Sutherland, Robert Duvall, Jenny Agutter and Donald Pleasence. Subsequently, in 1978, he starred in *The Silver Bears*, an adaptation of Paul Erdman's (1974) novel of the same name. Caine also was part of an all-star cast in *A Bridge Too Far* (1977).

1980s

By the end of the decade, he had moved to the United States, but his choice of roles was often criticised — he admitted to and has since made many self-deprecating comments about taking parts in numerous films he knew to be bad strictly for the money, despite working with Hollywood's highly regarded directors such as Irwin Allen, Richard Fleischer, Michael Ritchie and Oliver Stone. Caine was averaging two films a year, but these included such failures as the BAFTA Award-nominated *The Magus* (1968), the Academy Award-nominated *The Swarm* (1978), *Ashanti* (1979) (which he claimed were the worst three films of all the other worst films he ever made), *Beyond the Poseidon Adventure* (1979), *The Island* (1980), *The Hand* (1981) and a reunion with his *Sleuth* co-star Laurence Olivier in *The Jigsaw Man* (1982). Although Caine also took better roles, including a BAFTA-winning turn in *Educating Rita* (1983), and an Oscar-winning one in *Hannah and Her Sisters* (1986) and a Golden Globe-nominated one in *Dirty Rotten Scoundrels* (1988), he continued to appear in notorious duds like the financially-successful-but-critical-failure *Jaws: The Revenge* (1987) (in which he had mixed feelings about the production and the final cut) and *Bullseye!* (1990); his appearing in so many films that did not meet with critical or box office acclaim made him the butt of numerous jokes on the subject. Of the former, Caine famously said (primarily about *Jaws: The Revenge*) "I have never seen the film, but by all accounts it was terrible. However I have seen the house that it built, and it is terrific." All these film failures later became cult films among his fans today. His other successful films (either critically and/or financially) were the 1978 Academy Award-winning *California Suite*, the 1980 Golden Globe-nominated slasher film *Dressed to Kill*, the 1981 war film *Escape to Victory*, the 1982 film *Deathtrap*, and the 1986 Academy Award-nominated *Mona Lisa*. He also starred in *Without a Clue*, portraying Sherlock Holmes. 1989 A Shock to the System. Graham Marshall already celebrates his anxiously awaited promotion in an advertising company, when he learns that Roger Banham, one of his subordinates, will be promoted instead of him. Frustrated that his hated life will never change, he starts a cunning ploy to take revenge on everyone who humiliated him, starting with his unnerving wife.

1990s

The 1990s were a lean time for Caine, as he found good parts harder to come by. A high point came when he played Ebenezer Scrooge in the critically-acclaimed *Muppet Christmas Carol* (1992), which he considers to be one of his most memorable roles. He played the beleaguered stage director Lloyd Dallas in the film adaptation of *Noises Off* (1992). He also played a villain in the Steven Seagal film *On Deadly Ground* (1994). He was in two straight to video Harry Palmer sequels and a few television movies. However, Caine's reputation as a pop icon was still intact, thanks to his roles in films such as *The Italian Job* and *Get Carter*. His performance in 1998's *Little Voice* was seen as something of a return to form, and won him a Golden Globe Award. Better parts followed, including *The Cider House Rules* (1999), for which he won his second Oscar.

2000s

In the 2000s, Caine appeared in *Miss Congeniality* (2000), *Last Orders* (2001), *The Quiet American* (2002) and others that helped rehabilitate his reputation. Several of Caine's classic films have been remade, including *The Italian Job*, *Get Carter*, *Alfie* and *Sleuth*. In the 2007 remake of *Sleuth*, Caine took over the role Laurence Olivier played in the 1972 version and Jude Law played Caine's original role. Caine also starred in *Austin Powers: Goldmember* (2002) as Austin's father and in 2003 he co-starred with Robert Duvall in *Secondhand Lions*. In 2005, he was cast as Bruce Wayne's butler Alfred Pennyworth in the first production of the new *Batman* film series. In 2006, he appeared in the films *Children of Men* and *The Prestige*. In 2007 he appeared in *Flawless*, while in 2008 he reprised his role as Alfred in Christopher Nolan's critically acclaimed *Batman* sequel, *The Dark Knight* as well as starring in the British drama *Is Anybody There?*, which explores the final days of life.

It was reported by *Empire* magazine that Caine had said that *Harry Brown* (released on 13 November 2009) would be his last lead role. Caine later declared (in the *Daily Mirror*) that he had been misquoted by the magazine.

2010s

He appeared alongside Leonardo DiCaprio in Christopher Nolan's science fiction thriller, *Inception*.

Awards and honours

Caine has been Oscar-nominated six times, winning his first Academy Award for the 1986 film *Hannah and Her Sisters*, and his second in 1999 for *The Cider House Rules*, in both cases as a supporting actor. Caine is one of only two actors to be nominated for an Academy Award for acting (either lead or supporting) in every decade since the 1960s.[*citation needed*] The other is Jack Nicholson. The two actors starred together in the 1996 movie *Blood and Wine*.

He was appointed Commander of the Order of the British Empire (CBE) in the 1992 Queen's Birthday Honours, and in the 2000 New Year Honours he was knighted as *Sir Maurice Micklewhite, CBE*.

In 2008, he was awarded the prize for Outstanding Contribution to Showbusiness at the Variety Club Awards.

In popular culture

Caine is a popular subject for impressionists and mimics, having a voice and manner of speaking that are distinctive, yet fairly easy to imitate. Most Caine impressions include the catchphrase "Not a lot of people know that." Peter Sellers initiated this when he appeared on BBC1's *Parkinson* show on 28 October 1972 and said:

> Not many people know that. This is my Michael Caine impression. You see, Mike's always quoting from the *Guinness Book of Records*. At the drop of a hat he'll trot one out. 'Did you know that it takes a man in a tweed suit five and a half seconds to fall from the top of Big Ben to the ground?' Now there's not many people who know that!

The line had been used earlier in Spike Milligan's script for *The Last Goon Show of All*, performed on 5 October 1972.

In 1983, Caine was given the line to say as an in-joke in the film *Educating Rita*. The line was parodied in *Harry Enfield's Television Programme* by Paul Whitehouse, who introduced himself with the line "My name is Michael Paine, and I am a nosey neighbour." On 16 December 2007, Caine was the second guest on Michael Parkinson's *Final Conversation*.

Personal life

Caine lives near Leatherhead, Surrey, and is patron to the Leatherhead Drama Festival. He has also lived in North Stoke, Oxfordshire, Clewer near Windsor, Berkshire, Lowestoft in Suffolk and Chelsea Harbour in London. In addition, Caine owns a unit at The Apogee in Miami Beach, Florida. He still keeps a small flat near where he grew up in South East London. Caine published a volume of memoirs, *What's It All About?* in 1992 and told BBC Radio in 2010 he was preparing another, especially for aspiring actors [1].

He was married to actress Patricia Haines from 1955 to 1958. They had one daughter named Dominique. He dated Bianca Jagger in 1968. Caine has been married to actress and model Shakira Baksh since 8 January 1973. They met after Caine saw her appearing in a Maxwell House coffee commercial and a friend gave him her telephone number. They have a daughter named Natasha.

Caine with Scarlett Johansson at the Nobel Peace Prize Concert 2008.

Some time after his mother died, Caine and his younger brother, Stanley, learned they had an elder half-brother, named David. He suffered from severe epilepsy and had been kept in Cane Hill Mental Hospital his entire life. Although their mother regularly visited her first son in the hospital, even her husband did not know the child existed. David died in 1992.

Caine is a fan of Chelsea Football Club.[citation needed]

Trivia books written by Caine include *Not Many People Know That!*, *And Not Many People Know This Either!*, *Michael Caine's Moving Picture Show* and *Not A Lot of People Know This is 1988*. Proceeds from the books went to the National Playing Fields Association (now Fields In Trust) of which Caine was a prominent supporter.

Unlike many actors who adopt their stage name for everyday use, Caine still uses his real name when he is not working.[citation needed]

In the 2010 UK general election, Caine showed support for David Cameron and the Conservative Party, appearing alongside him at a press conference.

Caine was called up for national service in the British Army in 1951 when he was aged 18 and was deployed to South Korea to help in the aftermath of the North Korean invasion. He served as part of the Royal Fusiliers. He said he had gone into it feeling sympathetic to communism, coming as he did from a poor family. But he has said the experience left him permanently repelled.

Politics

Caine has been open about his political views. He left Britain in the 1970s, citing the 82% tax levied on top earners by the Labour government of the time, but returned to Britain several years later when taxes were lowered:

> *"I decided not to become a tax exile, so I stayed in Britain, but they kept putting the tax up, so I'd do any old thing every now and then to pay the tax, that was my tax exile money. I realised that's not a socialist country, it's a communist country without a dictator, so I left and I was never going to come back. Maggie Thatcher came in and put the taxes back down and in the end, you know, you don't mind paying tax. What am I going to do? Not pay tax and drive around in a Rolls Royce, with cripples begging on the street like you see in some countries?"*

> *"I voted for Maggie Thatcher because I thought we needed a change from that long period of socialism; I voted for Tony Blair because we had a great long period of Conservatism."*

In 2009, Caine openly criticised the Labour government's proposed new 50% tax on top earners:

> *"The Government has taken tax up to 50 per cent and if it goes to 51 I will be back in America. They have reached their limit with me and that's what will happen to a lot of people. You know how much they made out of that high taxation all those years ago? Nothing. But they sent a mass of incredible brains to America. We've got 3.5 million layabouts laying about on benefits, and I'm 76, getting up at 6am to go to work to keep them. Let's get everybody back to work so we can save a couple of billion and cut tax, not keep sticking it on."*

> *"You're saying to poor people, 'let's tax those rich gits' and I understand that. You slice up the cake, give everyone a chance, but don't destroy the people that are making the bloody cake! I really believe about taking care of people, I don't mind paying tax. It's how the government spends my tax that I detest, really detest, because I see the waste. More money than all our income tax is spent on benefits. Now you tell me there is nothing wrong with that system."*

Caine also stated in 2009 that he was likely to vote for the Conservatives again:

> *"I'll probably vote Conservative. I mean, we're in a terrible state whichever way you look at it, socially, financially and politically, so just give the other guy a chance. I don't know what Cameron's going to do, but in the end you vote out of desperation. You just have to have someone new and see what happens."*

Following the launch of his film *Harry Brown*, Caine called for the reintroduction of national service in the UK to give young people "a sense of belonging rather than a sense of violence".

During the run up to the 2010 General Election, Caine publicly endorsed Conservative Party policy regarding social exclusion.[*citation needed*]

Musical career

Caine is a fan of chillout music and has compiled a mix CD called *Cained*, which was released in 2007 by UMTV. According to Michael Caine, he met Elton John and was discussing musical tastes, when Caine claimed that he had been creating chillout mix tapes as an amateur for years. Also in music, Caine provided vocal samples for the band Madness for their 1984 hit "Michael Caine" as his daughter was a fan. He has sung in movie roles as well, including for the musical movie, *The Muppet Christmas Carol*.

Filmography, awards and nominations

Main article: Michael Caine filmography

External links

- The official Michael Caine website [2]
- Michael Caine [3] at the Internet Movie Database
- Michael Caine [4] at the British Film Institute's Screenonline
- PLAY DIRTY/Caine Special on Location in Spain [5]
- Martyn Palmer, "Double act: Michael Caine and Jude Law (lunch and discussion)", *The Times*, 17 November 2007 [6]
- Charlie Rose video interview 3 February 2003 [7]
- IGN.com interview 18 March 2003 [8]
- 200 years of Michael Caine's family tree [9]

1. REDIRECT Template:Navboxes

Professional Career - Filmography

Memento (film)

Memento	
Theatrical theatrical poster	
Directed by	Christopher Nolan
Produced by	Jennifer Todd Suzanne Todd
Screenplay by	Christopher Nolan
Story by	Jonathan Nolan
Starring	Guy Pearce Carrie-Anne Moss Joe Pantoliano
Music by	David Julyan
Cinematography	Wally Pfister
Editing by	Dody Dorn
Studio	Newmarket Capital Group Team Todd I Remember Productions Summit Entertainment
Distributed by	Summit Entertainment (USA) Pathé (UK from 2000-2010) E1 Entertainment (UK from 2011-present)
Release date(s)	**Venice International Film Festival:** September 5, 2000 **United States:** March 16, 2001
Running time	113 minutes
Country	United States
Language	English
Budget	$9 million

Gross revenue	$39,723,096

Memento is a 2000 American psychological thriller film written and directed by Christopher Nolan, adapted from his younger brother Jonathan's short story "Memento Mori". It stars Guy Pearce as Leonard Shelby, a man with anterograde amnesia which renders his brain unable to store new memories. During the opening credits, (which portrays the end of the story) it is shown that Leonard kills Teddy (Joe Pantoliano) for the rape and murder of his wife based on information provided by Natalie (Carrie-Anne Moss).

This film is often used to show the distinction between plot and story. The film's events unfold in two separate, alternating narratives — one in color, and the other in black and white. The black and white sections are told in chronological order, showing Leonard conversing with an anonymous phone caller in a motel room. Leonard's investigation is depicted in color sequences that are in reverse chronological order. As each sequence begins, the audience is unaware of the preceding events, just like Leonard, thereby giving the viewer a sense of his confusion. By the film's end when the two narratives converge we understand the investigation and the events that lead up to Teddy's death.

Memento premiered on September 5, 2000, at the Venice Film Festival to critical acclaim and received a similar response when it was released in European theaters starting in October 2000. Critics especially praised its unique, nonlinear narrative structure and themes of memory, perception, grief, self-deception, and revenge. The film was successful at the box office and received numerous accolades, including Academy Award nominations for Original Screenplay and Film Editing.

Plot

Memento is presented as two different sequences of scenes, a series in black-and-white that are shown chronologically, and a series of color sequences shown in reverse order. The two sequences "meet" at the end of the film, producing one common story. During the opening credits of the film, the only sequence to be played backwards is shown. It starts with the developed Polaroid photograph of a man shot in the head. As the sequence plays backwards we are shown the photo undeveloping, entering the camera, being taken, etc. As the credits end, we see the protagonist shoot a man in the head.

The movie starts in black-and-white with the protagonist, Leonard Shelby, in a motel room. Leonard has anterograde amnesia, impairing his ability to store memories of recent events. As Leonard explains in the film, his amnesia was a result of an attack by two men in his home. Leonard killed the attacker who raped and strangled his wife, but a second attacker clubbed him in the head and escaped. The police did not believe there was a second attacker, but Leonard has come to believe the attacker is a man known as "John G". During the black-and-white sequences we learn about Leonard's amnesia through the story Leonard tells an unnamed caller about the strange case of Sammy Jankis. Leonard explains how he met Sammy during his job as an insurance investigator. Sammy appeared to have anterograde amnesia after a car accident, but since Sammy could not learn through conditioning,

Leonard reported that Sammy's condition must be psychological rather than physical and therefore not covered. Leonard explains how Sammy's diabetic wife conducted her own experiment to try to test Sammy, repeatedly requesting her insulin injections hoping that Sammy would remember the previous injection. He didn't and, as a result, she fell into a coma, never recovering.

The color sequences, shown in reverse order starting with the opening murder, are about Leonard's investigation using his system of notes, Polaroid photos, and tattoos, to track down "John G". Leonard gets a tattoo, based on instructions to himself, identifying "John G."'s license plate. Finding a note in his clothes, he meets Natalie, a bartender. Natalie, seeing Leonard wearing the clothes and driving the car of her boyfriend, Jimmy, is at first resentful towards Leonard. After understanding his condition, and using this to get Leonard to drive a dangerous man named Dodd out of town, Natalie offers to run the license plate on Leonard's latest tattoo to help his investigation. Meanwhile, Leonard encounters another man, Teddy, who acts as Leonard's friend, helping him deal with Dodd, but warns him about Natalie; however, Leonard notes that his writing on the Polaroid of Teddy tells himself not to trust the man. Natalie eventually provides Leonard the driver's license, which matches that of John Edward Gammell — Teddy — and conforms with the rest of Leonard's information on "John G." and his Polaroid warnings. Leonard meets Teddy and drives him to an abandoned building, killing him as shown in the opening credits.

The climax of the film starts in the final black-and-white sequence. Prompted by the caller in the motel room, Leonard meets Teddy outside his motel. Teddy explains he is an undercover officer and has been helping Leonard with his investigation. Teddy says he's found Leonard's "John G." (Jimmy Grantz, Natalie's boyfriend) and directs Leonard to an abandoned building outside of town — the same location where Leonard will eventually kill him — and when Jimmy arrives, Leonard strangles him. Leonard takes a photo of the body and as this photo develops, the black-and-white scene transitions to color and the color sequences of the film begin.

Leonard swaps clothes with Jimmy and, as he drags the body to the basement, he hears Jimmy whisper "Sammy", causing Leonard to doubt that he really is the second attacker. When Teddy arrives and continues to assert that Jimmy was the John G. they've been looking for, Leonard refuses to trust him. Teddy admits that Jimmy was just a drug trafficker and that, together, they had already found and killed "the real John G" more than a year before. Teddy claims that Leonard has confused elements of his own life with that of Sammy, explaining that Sammy was a con artist who had no wife and that Leonard's own wife actually survived the attack and was herself diabetic and that it was Leonard's wife, not Mrs. Jankis, who died in an insulin overdose.

Teddy accuses Leonard of deliberately creating an unsolvable puzzle to give himself purpose. He points out that "John G." is a common enough name that Leonard's search can go on indefinitely. He reveals that even he has a "John G." name. In a conscious deliberate decision, Leonard burns the photograph of Jimmy's body and writes down Teddy's license plate number as a "fact" to be tattooed on himself as the second attacker's plate number. Leonard throws Teddy's keys into a bush and drives off in Jimmy's car. The film ends with Leonard stopping in front of a tattoo parlor, ready to get the license plate tattoo that will lead to Teddy's death.

Cast

- Guy Pearce as Leonard Shelby
- Carrie-Anne Moss as Natalie
- Joe Pantoliano as Teddy (John Edward Gammell)
- Mark Boone Junior as Burt
- Russ Fega as Waiter
- Jorja Fox as Leonard's Wife
- Stephen Tobolowsky as Sammy (Samuel R. Jankis)
- Harriet Sansom Harris as Mrs. Jankis
- Thomas Lennon as Doctor
- Callum Keith Rennie as Dodd
- Kimberly Campbell as Blonde
- Marianne Muellerleile as Tattooist
- Larry Holden as Jimmy (James F. Grantz)

Film structure

The film's fabula and sujet are very important in understanding the film. The sujet or the presentation of the film is structured with two timelines: one in color and one in black-and-white. The color sequences are alternated with black-and-white sequences. The black-and-white sequences are put together in the chronological order. The color ones, though shown forward (except for the very first one, which is shown in reverse) are ordered in reverse. Chronologically, the black-and-white sequences come first, the color sequences come next.

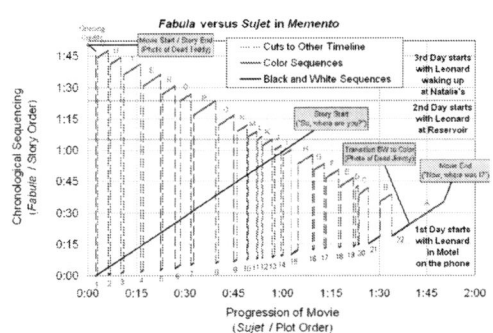

Fabula/Story vs Sujet/Plot.

Using the numbering scheme suggested by Andy Klein in his article for *Salon* magazine who took numbers from 1 to 22 for the black-and-white sequences and letters A-V for the color ones the plotting of the film as presented is: Opening Credits (shown "backwards"), 1, V, 2, U, 3, T, 4, S, ..., 22/A, Credits.

There is a smooth transition from the black-and-white sequence 22 to color sequence A and it occurs during the development of a polaroid photograph.

The fabula of the film (the chronological order of the story) can be viewed as a "Hidden feature" on the 2-Disc Limited Edition Region 1 DVD and the 3-Disc special Edition Region2 DVD. In this special feature the chapters of the film are put together into the chronological order and is shown: Ending Credits (run in reverse), 1, 2, 3, ..., 22, A, B, ..., V, then the opening title runs "backwards" to what was shown (the opening title sequence is run in reverse during the actual film, so it is shown forwards in this version).

Stefano Ghislotti wrote an article in *Film Anthology* which discusses how Nolan provides the viewer with the clues necessary to decode sujet/plotline as we watch and help us understand the fabula/story from it.

Production

Development

In July 1996, brothers Christopher and Jonathan Nolan took a cross-country road trip from Chicago to Los Angeles, as Christopher was relocating his home to the West Coast. During the drive, Jonathan pitched the story for the film to his brother, who responded enthusiastically to the idea. After they arrived in Los Angeles, Jonathan left for Washington, D.C., to finish college. Christopher repeatedly asked Jonathan to send him a first draft, and after a few months, Jonathan complied. Two months later, Christopher came up with the idea to tell the film backwards, and began to work on the screenplay. Jonathan wrote the short story simultaneously, and the brothers continued to correspond, sending each other subsequent revisions of their respective works.

Jonathan's short story, titled "Memento Mori", is radically different from Christopher's film, although it maintains the same essential elements. In Jonathan's version, Leonard is instead named Earl and is a patient at a mental institution. As in the film, his wife was killed by an anonymous man, and during the attack on his wife, Earl lost his short-term memory. Like Leonard, Earl leaves notes to himself and has tattoos with information about the killer. However, in the short story, Earl convinces himself through his own written notes to escape the mental institution and murder his wife's killer. Unlike the film, there is no ambiguity that Earl finds and kills the anonymous man.

In July 1997, Christopher's girlfriend Emma Thomas showed his screenplay to Aaron Ryder, an executive for Newmarket Films. Ryder said the script was, "perhaps the most innovative script I had ever seen", and soon after, it was optioned by Newmarket and given a budget of $4.5 million. Pre-production lasted seven weeks, during which the main shooting location changed from Montreal, Canada to Los Angeles, California, to create a more realistic and *noirish* atmosphere for the film.

Casting

Brad Pitt was initially slated to play the lead role of Leonard. Pitt was interested in the part, but passed due to scheduling conflicts. Other considered actors include Aaron Eckhart and Thomas Jane, but the role went to Guy Pearce, who impressed Nolan the most. Pearce was chosen partly for his "lack of celebrity" (after Pitt passed on the film, they "decided to eschew the pursuit of A-list stars and make the film for less money by using an affordable quality actor"), and his enthusiasm for the role, evidenced by a personal phone call Pearce made to Nolan to discuss the part.

After being impressed by Carrie-Anne Moss' performance as Trinity in the 1999 science fiction film *The Matrix*, Jennifer Todd suggested her for the part of Natalie. While Mary McCormack lobbied for the role, Nolan decided to cast Moss as Natalie, saying, "She added an enormous amount to the role of Natalie that wasn't on the page". For the corrupt police officer Teddy, Moss suggested her co-star from *The Matrix*, Joe Pantoliano. Although there was a concern that Pantoliano might be too villainous for the part, he was still cast, and Nolan said he was surprised by the actor's subtlety in his performance.

The rest of the film's characters were quickly cast after the three main leads were established. Stephen Tobolowsky and Harriet Sansom Harris play Sammy Jankis and his wife, respectively. Mark Boone Junior landed the role of Burt, the motel clerk, because Jennifer Todd liked his "look and attitude" for the part (as a result he has re-appeared in minor roles in other productions by Nolan). Larry Holden plays Jimmy Grantz, a drug dealer and Natalie's boyfriend, while Callum Keith Rennie performs the part of Dodd, a thug to whom Jimmy owes money. Rounding out the cast is Jorja Fox as Leonard's wife and Kimberly Campbell as a prostitute.

Filming

Filming took place from September 7 to October 8, 1999, a 25-day shooting schedule. Pearce was on set every day during filming, although all three principal actors (including Pantoliano and Moss) only performed together the first day, shooting exterior sequences outside Natalie's house. All of Moss' scenes were completed in the first week, including follow-up scenes at Natalie's home, Ferdy's bar, and the restaurant where she meets Leonard for the final time.

Pantoliano returned to the set late in the second week to continue filming his scenes. On September 25, the crew shot the opening scene in which Leonard kills Teddy. Although the scene is in reverse motion, Nolan used forward-played sounds. For a shot of a shell casing flying upwards, the shell had to be dropped in front of the camera in forward motion, but it constantly rolled out of frame. Nolan was forced to blow the casing out of frame instead, but in the confusion, the crew shot it backwards. They then had to make an optical (a copy of the shot) and reverse the shot to make it go forward again. "That was the height of complexity in terms of the film", Nolan says. "An optical to make a backwards running shot forwards, and the forwards shot is a simulation of a backwards shot."

The next day, on September 26, Larry Holden returned to shoot the sequence where Leonard attacks Jimmy. After filming was completed five days later, Pearce's voice-overs were recorded. For the black-and-white scenes, Pearce was given free rein to improvise his narrative, allowing for a documentary feel.

The Travel Inn in Tujunga, California, was repainted and used as Leonard's and Dodd's motel rooms. Scenes in Sammy Jankis' house were shot in a suburban home close to Pasadena, while Natalie's house was located in Burbank. The crew planned to shoot the derelict building set (where Leonard kills Teddy and Jimmy) in a Spanish-styled brick building owned by a train company. However, one week before shooting began, the company placed several dozen train carriages outside the building, making the exterior unfilmable. Since the interior of the building had already been built as a set, a new location had to be found. An oil refinery near Long Beach was used instead, and the scene where Leonard burns his wife's possessions was filmed on the other side of the refinery.

Music

David Julyan composed the film's synthesized score. Julyan acknowledges several synthesized soundtracks that inspired him, such as Vangelis' *Blade Runner* and Hans Zimmer's *The Thin Red Line*. While composing the score, Julyan created different, distinct sounds to differentiate between the color and black-and-white scenes: "brooding and classical" themes in the former, and "oppressive and rumbly noise" in the latter. Since he describes the entire score as "Leonard's theme", Julyan says, "The emotion I was aiming at with my music was yearning and loss. But a sense of loss you feel but at the same time you don't know what it is you have lost, a sense of being adrift." Initially, Nolan wanted to use Radiohead's "Paranoid Android" during the end credits, but he was unable to secure the rights. Instead, David Bowie's "Something in the Air" is used, although another of Radiohead's songs, an extended version of "Treefingers", is included on the film's soundtrack.

Releases

The film gained substantial word-of-mouth press from the film festival circuit. It premiered at the 2000 Venice Film Festival, where it received a standing ovation, and afterwards played at Deauville Festival of American Film and the Toronto Film Festival. With the publicity from these events, *Memento* did not have trouble finding foreign distributors, opening in more than 20 countries worldwide. Its promotion tour ended at the Sundance Film Festival, where it played in January 2001.

Finding American distributors proved more troublesome. *Memento* was screened for various studio heads (including Miramax chief Harvey Weinstein) in March 2000. Although most of the executives loved the film and praised Nolan's talent, all passed on distributing the picture, believing it was too confusing and would not attract a large audience. After famed independent film director Steven Soderbergh saw the film and learned it was not being distributed, he championed the film in interviews and public events, giving it even more publicity, although he did not secure a distributor. Newmarket, in a financially risky move, decided to distribute the film itself. After the first few weeks of distribution, *Memento* had reached more than 500 theaters and earned a domestic total of $25 million in its box-office run. The film's success was surprising to those who passed on the film, so much so that Weinstein realized his mistake and tried to buy the film from Newmarket.

Marketing

Jonathan Nolan designed the film's official website. As with the marketing strategy of *The Blair Witch Project*, the website was intended to provide further clues and hints to the story, while not providing any concrete information. After a short intro on the website, the viewer is shown a newspaper clipping detailing Leonard's murder of Teddy. Clicking on highlighted words in the article leads to more material describing the film, including Leonard's notes and photographs as well as police reports. The filmmakers employed another tactic by sending out Polaroid pictures to random people, depicting a bloody and shirtless Leonard pointing at an unmarked spot on his chest. Since Newmarket distributed the film themselves, Christopher Nolan edited the film's trailers himself. Sold to inexpensive cable-TV channels like Bravo and A&E, and websites such as Yahoo and MSN, the trailers were key to the film gaining widespread public notice.

Home media

Memento was released on DVD and VHS in the United States and Canada on September 4, 2001, and in the United Kingdom on January 14, 2002. The UK edition contains a hidden feature that allows the viewer to watch the film in chronological order. The Canadian version does not have this feature but the film chapters are set up to do this manually or through DVD programming. The original US release does not have the chronological feature nor are the chapters set up correctly to do it.

The film was later re-released in a limited edition DVD that features an audio commentary by Christopher Nolan, the original short story by Jonathan Nolan on which the film was based, and a Sundance Channel documentary on the making of the film. The limited edition DVD also contains a hidden feature that allows the viewer to watch the film in chronological order.

The Limited Edition DVD is uniquely packaged to look like Leonard's case file from a mental institution, with notes scribbled by "doctors" and Leonard on the inside. The DVD menus are designed as a series of psychological tests; the viewer has to choose certain words, objects, and multiple choice answers to play the movie or access special features. Leonard's "notes" on the DVD case offer clues to navigating the DVD.

Memento was re-released in the UK on a 3-disc Special Edition DVD on December 27, 2004. This release contains all the special features that are on the two US releases in one package plus a couple of new interviews. The menus appear as tattoos on a body and are more straightforward than the US 2-disc limited edition DVD.

Memento was released on Blu-ray Disc on August 15, 2006. This release lacks the special features contained on the Limited Edition DVD, but does include the audio commentary by director Christopher Nolan. The single-layer disc features an MPEG-2 1080p transfer and PCM 5.1 surround audio. The film was also released on iTunes as a digital download.

Reception

Memento was a box office success. During its opening weekend, it was released in only 11 theaters, but by week 11 it was distributed to more than 500 theaters. It grossed $25,544,867 in North America and $14,178,229 in foreign countries, making the film's total worldwide gross some $40 million as of August 2007. During its theatrical run, it did not place higher than eighth in the list of highest-grossing movies for a single weekend.

The film was nominated for Academy Awards in Original Screenplay and Editing, but did not win in either category. Because Jonathan Nolan's short story was not published before the film was released, it was nominated for Original Screenplay instead of Adapted Screenplay. It was also nominated for the Grand Jury Prize at the Sundance Film Festival, but lost to *The Believer*. However, it won 13 awards for Best Screenplay and five awards for Best Picture from various film critic associations and festivals, including the Chicago Film Critics Association and the Sundance Waldo Salt Screenwriting Award. Christopher Nolan was nominated for three Best Director awards including the Directors Guild of America Award and was awarded one from the Independent Spirit Awards. Guy Pearce was accorded Best Actor from the San Diego Film Critics Society and the Las Vegas Film Critics Society.

Critical response

Memento was met with near universal critical acclaim, earning a 93% rating on Rotten Tomatoes, a website that aggregates professional critiques. Online film critic James Berardinelli gave the film four out of four stars, ranking it number one on his year-end Top Ten list and number sixty-three on his All-Time Top 100 films. In his review, he called it an "endlessly fascinating, wonderfully open-ended motion picture [that] will be remembered by many who see it as one of the best films of the year". Berardinelli praised the film's backwards narrative, saying that "what really distinguishes this film is its brilliant, innovative structure", and noted that Guy Pearce gives an "astounding...tight, and thoroughly convincing performance". In 2009, Berardinelli chose *Memento* as his #3 best movie of the decade. William Arnold of the *Seattle Post-Intelligencer* writes that *Memento* is a "delicious one-time treat", and emphasizes that director Christopher Nolan "not only makes *Memento* work as a non-linear puzzle film, but as a tense, atmospheric thriller". Rob Blackwelder noted that "Nolan has a crackerjack command over the intricacies of this story. He makes every single element of the film a clue to the larger picture...as the story edges back toward the origins of [Leonard's] quest".

However, not all critics were impressed with the film's structure. Marjorie Baumgarten wrote, "In forward progression, the narrative would garner little interest, thus making the reverse storytelling a filmmaker's conceit." Sean Burns of the *Philadelphia Weekly* commented that "For all its formal wizardry, Memento is ultimately an ice-cold feat of intellectual gamesmanship. Once the visceral thrill of the puzzle structure begins to wear off, there's nothing left to hang onto. The film itself fades like one of Leonard's temporary memories". While Roger Ebert gave the film a favorable three out of four stars, he did not think it warranted multiple viewings. After watching *Memento* twice, he concluded that "Greater understanding helped on the plot level, but didn't enrich the viewing experience. Confusion is the state we are intended to be in". Jonathan Rosenbaum disliked the film, and commented in his review of *Eternal Sunshine of the Spotless Mind* that *Memento* is a "gimmicky and unpoetic counterfeit."

Scientific response

Many medical experts have cited *Memento* as one of the most realistic and accurate depictions of anterograde amnesia in any motion picture. Caltech neuroscientist Christof Koch called *Memento* "the most accurate portrayal of the different memory systems in the popular media," while physician Esther M. Sternberg, Director of the Integrative Neural Immune Program at the National Institute of Mental Health identified the film as "close to a perfect exploration of the neurobiology of memory." Sternberg concludes: "This thought-provoking thriller is the kind of movie that keeps reverberating in the viewer's mind, and each iteration makes one examine preconceived notions in a different light. *Memento* is a movie for anyone interested in the workings of memory and, indeed, in what it is that makes our own reality."

Clinical neuropsychologist Sallie Baxendale writes in *Memories aren't made of this: amnesia at the movies*: "The overwhelming majority of amnesic characters in films bear little relation to any neurological or psychiatric realities of memory loss... Apparently inspired partly by the neuropsychological studies of the famous patient HM (who developed severe anterograde memory impairment after neurosurgery to control his epileptic seizures) and the temporal lobe amnesic syndrome, the film documents the difficulties faced by Leonard, who develops a severe anterograde amnesia after an attack in which his wife is killed. Unlike in most films in this genre, this amnesic character retains his identity, has little retrograde amnesia, and shows several of the severe everyday memory difficulties associated with the disorder. The fragmented, almost mosaic quality to the sequence of scenes in the film also reflects the 'perpetual present' nature of the syndrome."

Lists of the best films

Year	Presenter	Title	Rank	Note
2009	*The Onion A.V. Club*	The Best Films of the '00s	5	
2008	*Empire*	The 500 Greatest Movies of All Time	173	
2005	Internet Movie Database (IMDb)	15th Anniversary Top 15 Films for the Last 15 Years	7	
2003	*1001 Movies You Must See Before You Die*		None	
2001	National Board of Review (NBR)	Top 10 Films of the Year		
2001	American Film Institute (AFI)			

See also

- Personal identity (philosophy)
- Henry Molaison ("patient HM")

Memory

- Anterograde amnesia
- Long-term memory
- Short-term memory
- Working memory
- Episodic memory
- False memories

References

- Mottram, James. *The Making of Memento*. New York: Faber, 2002. ISBN 0571214886.

External links

- Official website [1]
- *Memento* [2] at the Internet Movie Database
- *Memento* [3] at Allmovie
- *Memento* [4] at Rotten Tomatoes
- *Memento* [4] at Box Office Mojo
- A detailed analysis [5] of the film by Andy Klein at Salon.com
- Interview: Christopher Nolan [6] by the Onion AV Club
- Review of Memento [7] by the Onion AV Club

- Plot Holes: Memento [8], a musing on how certain discrepancies might be plot holes or of more significance, on Slate
- Memento and anterograde amnesia [9]
- Metacritic: *Memento* [10]
- Cinematographic analysis of Memento [11]
- Blu-ray info, screenshots and review [12]

Batman Begins

Batman Begins	
Theatrical release poster	
Directed by	Christopher Nolan
Produced by	Emma Thomas Larry J. Franco Charles Roven
Screenplay by	David S. Goyer Christopher Nolan
Story by	David S. Goyer Bob Kane (comic book) Bill Finger (comic book)
Starring	Christian Bale Michael Caine Liam Neeson Katie Holmes Gary Oldman Cillian Murphy Morgan Freeman
Music by	Hans Zimmer James Newton Howard
Cinematography	Wally Pfister
Editing by	Lee Smith
Studio	DC Comics Legendary Pictures Syncopy Films
Distributed by	Warner Bros.
Release date(s)	June 10, 2005 (Russia) June 15, 2005
Running time	139 minutes
Country	United States
Language	English
Budget	$150 million
Gross revenue	$372,710,015

Followed by	*The Dark Knight*

Batman Begins is a 2005 superhero film based on the fictional DC Comics character Batman, directed by Christopher Nolan. It stars Christian Bale as Batman, along with Michael Caine, Gary Oldman, Liam Neeson, Katie Holmes, Cillian Murphy, Morgan Freeman, Ken Watanabe, Tom Wilkinson, and Rutger Hauer. The film reboots the *Batman* film series, telling the origin story of the character and begins with Bruce Wayne's initial fear of bats, the death of his parents, and his journey to becoming Batman. It draws inspiration from classic comic book storylines such as *The Man Who Falls*, *Batman: Year One*, and *Batman: The Long Halloween*.

After a series of unsuccessful projects to resurrect Batman on screen following the 1997 critical failure of *Batman & Robin*, Nolan and David S. Goyer began work on the film in early 2003 and aimed for a darker and more realistic tone, with humanity and realism being the basis of the film. The goal was to get the audience to care for both Batman and Bruce Wayne. The film, which was primarily shot in England and Chicago, relied on traditional stunts and miniatures—computer-generated imagery was used minimally. A new Batmobile (called the Tumbler) and a more mobile Batsuit were both created specifically for the film.

Batman Begins was critically and commercially successful. The film opened on June 15, 2005 in the United States and Canada in 3,858 theaters. It grossed $48 million in its opening weekend, eventually grossing over $372 million worldwide. The film received an 84% overall approval rating from Rotten Tomatoes. Critics noted that fear was a common theme throughout the film, and remarked that it had a darker tone compared to previous *Batman* films. A sequel titled *The Dark Knight* was released in July 2008 and also saw the return of both Nolan and Bale to the franchise.

Plot

A young Bruce Wayne falls down a well and is attacked by bats. Bruce then awakens from this nightmare of his past and is revealed to be a prisoner in Bhutan. He is approached by Henri Ducard, who speaks for Ra's al Ghul, leader of the League of Shadows, and invites him to train with the elite vigilante group. The narrative returns to Bruce's childhood, to the fateful night he witnessed his parents' murder by a mugger named Joe Chill. Chill is later arrested and Bruce is taken home and raised by the family butler Alfred Pennyworth.

Years later, Bruce returns to Gotham City from Princeton University, intent on killing Chill, whose prison sentence is being suspended in exchange for testifying against crime boss Carmine Falcone. Before he can act, however, one of Falcone's assassins kills Chill. Rachel Dawes, Bruce's childhood friend and now an assistant district attorney, is disgusted with Bruce's intent, telling him his father would be ashamed of him. That night, Bruce confronts Falcone, who tells the young man that his criminal empire is invincible because it runs on fear. Inspired, Bruce decides to travel the world for several years, learning the various ways of the criminal underworld, before himself becoming a criminal and being arrested. After Bruce's training in the League of Shadows, Ra's and Ducard tell Bruce his purpose: He must lead the League to destroy Gotham, which they believe is corrupt beyond saving. Bruce refuses to become a murderer and battles Ra's, burning the temple in the process, before making his escape. Ra's is killed by falling debris, but Bruce saves an unconscious Ducard and returns to Gotham.

Falcone now dominates the city. Bruce enlists the help of Sgt. Jim Gordon, one of the city's few honest police officers, and befriends Lucius Fox, a former board member of Wayne Enterprises. Fox helps Bruce acquire a prototype armored car and an experimental armored suit. With Alfred, Bruce finds another entrance to the cave under the well and creates a workshop, modifying his equipment to take up the identity of Batman. On his first night out as a vigilante, he intercepts a drug shipment, captures Falcone and provides Rachel with the evidence to indict him. Falcone and his men are transferred to Arkham Asylum with the help of the hospital's corrupt administrator, Dr. Jonathan Crane, who has been paying off Falcone to ship a toxic hallucinogenic into Gotham City; Crane uses the toxin in his experiments, using his patients as guinea pigs. When Falcone demands a bigger share, Crane gasses Falcone with the same toxin, literally driving him insane with fear. While investigating the drugs, Batman encounters Crane, who also sprays him with the fear toxin. Alfred rescues him, using an anti-toxin developed by Fox. Crane later summons Rachel to Arkham and shows her that the toxin has been introduced into Gotham's water supply from Arkham for weeks, and then infects her. Batman doses Crane with the toxin, saves Rachel, and then takes her to his cave giving her vials for Gordon: One for inoculating himself and the other for mass production.

At Bruce's birthday celebration at Wayne Manor, he is confronted by Ducard, who reveals himself to be the real Ra's al Ghul, and has now arrived in Gotham personally to destroy the city; he had conspired with Crane to poison Gotham's water supply with the toxin, vaporizing it with a stolen device from Wayne Enterprises. After Bruce pretends to be drunk to get everyone to leave, he and Ra's fight. Ra's' men burn down the mansion, release all the inmates at Arkham, and vaporize the hallucinogen into the atmosphere. Although Wayne Manor is destroyed, Bruce escapes the inferno with help from Alfred. Rachel delivers the antidote to Gordon and wards off Crane, now calling himself Scarecrow, with a taser. Batman reveals his identity to Rachel and then has Gordon drive the Batmobile to Wayne Tower, the central hub of the Gotham elevated rail system. Ra's boards the train; his objective is to reach Wayne Tower with the vaporizer as it is also a major water hub. As Batman confronts Ra's on the train, Gordon destroys the elevated tracks. Batman jams the controls and escapes the train as it crashes, leaving Ra's to die.

Following the battle, Batman becomes a public hero and Bruce gains control of his company; he fires the former CEO, William Earle, and replaces him with Lucius Fox. However, he loses Rachel, who cannot bring herself to love both Bruce and Batman. Gordon, now a Lieutenant, shows Batman the Bat-Signal and mentions a new criminal who leaves Joker playing cards at crime scenes. Batman promises to investigate, and disappears into the night.

Cast

- Christian Bale as Bruce Wayne / Batman: Wayne is a billionaire industrialist whose parents were killed by a mugger when he was eight years old. Traveling the world for several years to seek the means to fight injustice, he returns to Gotham. At night, Bruce becomes Batman, Gotham City's vigilante protector. Bale was cast on September 11, 2003, having expressed interest in playing Batman since Darren Aronofsky was planning his own film adaptation. Some of the early candidates for the Batman/Bruce Wayne role were Billy Crudup, Jake Gyllenhaal, Hugh Dancy, Joshua Jackson, Eion Bailey, and Cillian Murphy. Bale felt the previous films underused Batman's character, overplaying the villains instead. To best pose as Batman, Bale studied graphic novels and illustrations of the superhero. David Boreanaz was the first choice for the role before Bale.

Director Nolan said of Bale, "He has exactly the balance of darkness and light that we were looking for." Goyer stated that while some actors could play a great Bruce Wayne or a great Batman, Bale could portray both radically different personalities. Bale described the part as playing four characters: the raging Batman persona; the shallow playboy façade Bruce uses to ward off suspicion; the vengeful young man; and the older, angrier Bruce who is discovering his purpose in life. Bale's dislike of his costume, which heated up regularly, helped him get into a necessarily foul mood. He said, "Batman's meant to be fierce, and you become a beast in that suit, as Batman should be — not a man in a suit, but a different creature."

Since he had lost a great deal of weight in preparation for his role in *The Machinist*, Bale hired a personal trainer to help him gain 100 pounds (45 kg) in the span of only a couple of months to help him physically prepare for the role. He first went well over the weight required and created concern over whether he would look right for the part. Bale recognized that his large physique was not appropriate for Batman, who relies on speed and strategy. He lost the excess weight by the time filming began. The role of Bruce Wayne at age eight was portrayed by Gus Lewis.

- Michael Caine as Alfred Pennyworth: The trusted butler to Bruce Wayne's parents, who continues his loyal service to their son after their deaths. He is Bruce Wayne's closest confidant. Nolan felt Caine would effectively portray the foster father element of the character. Although Alfred's family is depicted in the film as having served the Wayne family for generations, Caine created his own backstory, in that before becoming Wayne's butler, Alfred served in the Special Air Service. After being wounded, he was invited to the position of the Wayne family butler by Thomas Wayne because, "He wanted a butler, but someone a bit tougher than that, you know?"

- Liam Neeson as Henri Ducard: In reality Ra's al Ghul in disguise and the main antagonist of the film, Ducard trains Bruce in ninjutsu, a form of martial arts. Writer David Goyer said he felt Ra's was the most complex of all the Batman villains, comparing him to Osama bin Laden; "He's not crazy in the way that all the other Batman villains are. He's not bent on revenge; he's actually trying to heal the world. He's just doing it by very draconian means." Neeson is commonly cast as a mentor, so the revelation that his character was the main villain was intended to shock viewers.

- Katie Holmes as Rachel Dawes: Bruce's childhood friend who serves as Gotham City's assistant district attorney, fighting against the corruption in the city. Nolan found a "tremendous warmth and great emotional appeal" in Holmes, and also felt "she has a maturity beyond her years that comes across in the film and is essential to the idea that Rachel is something of a moral conscience for Bruce". Sarah Michelle Gellar and Rachel McAdams were in the running for the role. Emma Lockhart portrays the young Rachel Dawes.

- Gary Oldman as Sgt. James Gordon: One of the few uncorrupted Gotham City police officers. He was the officer on duty the night of the murder of Bruce Wayne's parents. In this way, he shares a special bond with the adult Bruce and thus with Batman. Nolan originally wanted to cast Oldman as a villain, but when Chris Cooper turned down the role of Gordon to spend time with his family he decided that it would be refreshing for Oldman to play the role instead. "I embody the themes of the movie which are the values of family, courage and compassion and a sense of right and wrong, good and bad and justice," Oldman said of his character. Oldman filmed most of his scenes in Britain. Goyer said Oldman heavily resembled Gordon as drawn by David Mazzucchelli in *Batman: Year One*.

- Cillian Murphy as Dr. Jonathan Crane / The Scarecrow: A psychopharmacologist who works at Arkham Asylum and has developed fear-inducing toxins. He takes on the persona of the Scarecrow to use during his experiments, in which he uses his patients as human guinea pigs for his toxins. He is the primary antagonist and works with Ra's al Ghul and Carmine Falcone. Nolan decided against Irish actor Murphy for Batman, before casting him as Scarecrow. Murphy read numerous comics featuring the Scarecrow, and discussed making the character look less theatrical with Nolan. Murphy explained, "I wanted to avoid the Worzel Gummidge look, because he's not a very physically imposing man — he's more interested in the manipulation of the mind and what that can do."

- Tom Wilkinson as Carmine Falcone: The ruler of the Gotham City underworld. He had shared a prison cell with Joe Chill after Joe murdered Wayne's parents. He had Chill murdered when he decided to testify against Falcone. He goes into business with Dr. Jonathan Crane and Ra's al Ghul by smuggling a fear toxin through a shipment and putting it in the city's water supply.

- Morgan Freeman as Lucius Fox: A high-ranking Wayne Enterprises employee who was demoted to working in the company's Applied Science Division, where he conducts advanced studies in biochemistry and mechanical engineering. Fox supplies Bruce with much of the gear necessary to carry out Batman's mission and is promoted to CEO when Bruce repossesses the company by the end of the film. Freeman was Goyer's first and only choice for the role.

Other cast members include Rutger Hauer as William Earle, the CEO of Wayne Enterprises who takes the company public in the long-term absence of Bruce Wayne; Mark Boone Junior as Gordon's corrupt partner Detective Arnold Flass; Ken Watanabe as Ra's al Ghul's decoy; Larry Holden as district attorney Finch; Colin McFarlane as Police commissioner Gillian B. Loeb; Linus Roache and Sara

Stewart as Thomas and Martha Wayne, Bruce's parents; Richard Brake as Joe Chill, the Waynes' killer; Gerard Murphy as the corrupt High Court Judge Faden; Tim Booth as Victor Zsasz; Rade Šerbedžija as a homeless man, who is the last person to meet Bruce when he leaves Gotham, and the first civilian to see Batman, and Andrew Pleavin as a uniformed policeman. Actors John Foo and Mark Strange appear as members of the League of Shadows Warriors.

Production

Development

Further information: Batman in film#Proposals for fifth film

In January 2003, Warner Bros. hired *Memento* director Christopher Nolan to direct an untitled *Batman* film, and David S. Goyer signed on to write the script two months later. Nolan stated his intention to reinvent the film franchise of Batman by "doing the origins story of the character, which is a story that's never been told before". Nolan said that humanity and realism would be the basis of the origin film, and that "the world of Batman is that of grounded reality. [It] will be a recognizable, contemporary reality against which an extraordinary heroic figure arises." Goyer said that the goal of the film was to get the audience to care for both Batman and Bruce Wayne. Nolan felt the previous films were exercises in style rather than drama, and described his inspiration as being Richard Donner's 1978 film *Superman*, in its focus on depicting the character's growth. Also similar to *Superman*, Nolan wanted an all-star supporting cast for *Batman Begins* to lend a more epic feel and credibility to the story.

Nolan's personal "jumping off point" of inspiration was "Batman: The Man Who Falls", a short story by Denny O'Neil and Dick Giordano about Bruce's travels throughout the world. The early scene in *Batman Begins* of young Bruce Wayne falling into a well was adapted from "The Man Who Falls". *Batman: The Long Halloween*, written by Jeph Loeb and drawn by Tim Sale, influenced Goyer in writing the screenplay, with the villain Carmine Falcone as one of many elements which were drawn from *Halloween*'s "sober, serious approach". The writers considered having Harvey Dent in the film, but replaced him with the new character Rachel Dawes when they realized they "couldn't do him justice". The character was later portrayed by Aaron Eckhart in the 2008 sequel *The Dark Knight*. The sequel to *Halloween*, *Batman: Dark Victory*, also served as an influence. Goyer used the vacancy of Bruce Wayne's multi-year absence presented in *Batman: Year One* to help set up some of the film's events in the transpiring years. In addition, the film's Sergeant James Gordon was based on his comic book incarnation as seen in *Year One*. The writers of *Batman Begins* also used Frank Miller's *Year One* plot device, which was about a corrupt police force that led to Gordon and Gotham City's need for Batman.

A common idea in the comics is that Bruce saw a Zorro film with his parents before they were murdered. Nolan explained that by ignoring that idea — which he stated is not found in Batman's first appearances — it emphasized the importance of bats to Bruce and that becoming a superhero is a wholly original idea on his part. It is for this reason Nolan believes other DC characters do not exist in the universe of his film; otherwise, Wayne's reasons for taking up costumed vigilantism would have been very different.

Filming

As with all his films, Nolan refused a second unit to keep his vision consistent. Filming began in March 2004 in the Vatnajökull glacier in Iceland (standing in for Bhutan). The crew built a village and the front doors to Ra's temple, as well as a road to access the remote area. The weather was problematic, with 75 miles per hour (121 km/h) winds, rain, and a lack of snow. A shot Wally Pfister had planned with a crane had to be done with a handheld camera.

In seeking inspiration from *Superman* and other blockbuster films of the late 1970s and early 1980s, Nolan based most of the production in England, specifically Shepperton Studios. A Batcave set was built there and measured 250 feet (76 m) long, 120 feet (37 m) wide, and 40 feet (12 m) high. Production designer Nathan Crowley installed twelve pumps to create a waterfall with 12000 imperial gallons (55000 l; 14000 US gal), and built rocks using molds of real caves. In January 2004, an airship hangar at Cardington, Bedfordshire was rented by Warner Bros. for filming in April 2004. There, the Narrows and the feet of the monorails filled the 900 feet (270 m) long stage.

Mentmore Towers was chosen from twenty different locations for Wayne Manor, as Nolan and Crowley liked its white floors, which gave the impression of the manor as a memorial to Wayne's parents. The building chosen to represent Arkham Asylum was the National Institute for Medical Research building in Mill Hill, northwest London, England. The St. Pancras railway station and the Abbey Mills Pumping Stations were used for Arkham's interiors. The University College London was used for courtrooms. Some scenes, including the Batmobile pursuit, were filmed in Chicago at locations such as Lower Wacker Drive and 35 East Wacker. Authorities agreed to raise Franklin Street Bridge for a scene where access to the Narrows is closed.

Despite the film's darkness, Nolan wanted to make the film appeal to a wide age range. "Not the youngest kids obviously, I think what we've done is probably a bit intense for them but I certainly didn't want to exclude the sort of ten to 12-year olds, because as a kid I would have loved to have seen a movie like this." Because of this, nothing gory or bloody was filmed.

Design

Nolan used the 1982 cult science fiction film *Blade Runner* as a source of inspiration for *Batman Begins*. He screened *Blade Runner* to cinematographer Wally Pfister and two others to show the attitude and style that he wanted to draw from the film. Nolan described the film's world as "an interesting lesson on the technique of exploring and describing a credible universe that doesn't appear to have any boundaries", a lesson that he applied to the production of *Batman Begins*.

Nolan worked with production designer Nathan Crowley to create the look of Gotham City. Crowley built a model of the city that filled Nolan's garage. Crowley and Nolan designed it as a large, modern metropolitan area that would reflect the various periods of architecture that the city had gone through. Elements were drawn from New York City, Chicago, and Tokyo; the latter for its elevated freeways and monorails. The Narrows was based on the slummish nature of the (now demolished) walled city of Kowloon in Hong Kong.

Batmobile

See also: Batmobile

Crowley started the process of designing the Tumbler for the film by model bashing. Crowley used the nose cone of a P-38 Lightning model to serve as the chassis for the Tumbler's turbine engine. Six models of the Tumbler were built to 1:12 scale in the course of four months. Following the scale model creation, a crew of over 30 people, including Crowley and engineers Chris Culvert and Annie Smith, carved a full-size replica of the Tumbler out of a large block of Styrofoam in two months.

The Tumbler, the Batmobile used in
Batman Begins

The Styrofoam model was used to create a steel "test frame", which had to stand up to several standards: have a speed of over 100 miles per hour (160 km/h), go from 0 to 60 miles per hour (97 km/h) in 5 seconds, possess a steering system to make sharp turns at city corners, and withstand a self-propelled launch of up to 30 feet (9.1 m). On the first jump test, the Tumbler's front end collapsed and had to be completely rebuilt. The basic configuration of the newly designed Tumbler included a 8.7-liter Chevy V8 engine, a truck axle for the rear axle, front tires by Hoosier (which are actually dirt racing tires used on the right rear of open wheel sprint cars), rear 4x4 mud tires by Interco., and the suspension system of Baja racing trucks. The design and development process took nine months and cost several million dollars.

The rear of the Tumbler, showing the flaps
and engine

With the design process complete, four street-ready race cars were constructed, with each vehicle possessing 65 panels and costing $250,000 to build. Two of the four cars were specialized versions. One version was the flap version, which had hydraulics and flaps to detail the close-up shots where the vehicle propelled itself through the air. The other version was the jet version, in which an actual jet engine was mounted onto the vehicle, fueled by six propane tanks. Due to the poor visibility inside the vehicle by the driver, monitors were connected to cameras on the vehicle body. The professional drivers for the Tumblers practiced driving the vehicles for six months before they drove on the streets of Chicago for the film's scenes.

The interior of the Tumbler was an immobile studio set and not actually the interior of a street-capable Tumbler. The cockpit was over-sized to fit cameras for scenes filmed in the Tumbler interior. In addition, another version of the Tumbler was a miniature model that was 1:5 scale of the actual Tumbler. This miniature model had an electric motor and was used to show the Tumbler flying across ravines and between buildings. However, the actual Tumbler was used for the waterfall sequence.

Batsuit

The filmmakers intended to create a very mobile Batsuit that would allow the wearer to move easily to fight and crouch. Previous film incarnations of the Batsuit had been stiff and especially restricted full head movement. Costume designer Lindy Hemming and her crew worked on the Batsuit at an FX workshop codenamed "Cape Town", a secured compound located at Shepperton Studios in London. The Batsuit's basic design was a neoprene undersuit, which was shaped by attaching molded cream latex sections. Christian Bale was molded and sculpted prior to his physical training so the team could work on a full body cast. To avoid imperfections picked up by sculpting with clay, plastiline was used to smooth the surface. In addition, the team brewed different mixtures of foam to find the mixture that would be the most flexible, light, durable, and black. The latter presented a problem, since the process to make the foam black reduced the foam's durability.

For the cape, director Christopher Nolan wanted to have a "flowing cloak... that blows and flows as in so many great graphic novels". Hemming's team created the cape out of their own version of parachute nylon that had electrostatic flocking, a process shared with the team by the British Ministry of Defence. The process was used by the London police force to minimize night vision detection. The cape was topped by a cowl, which was designed by Nolan, Hemming, and costume effects supervisor Graham Churchyard. The cowl was created to be thin enough to allow motion but thick enough to avoid wrinkling when Bale turned his head in the Batsuit. Churchyard explained the cowl had been designed to show "a man who has angst", so his character would be revealed through the mask.

Special effects

For *Batman Begins*, Nolan preferred using traditional stuntwork over computer generated imagery. Scale models were used to represent the Narrows and Ra's al Ghul's temple. There were, however, several establishing shots that were CG composite images; that is, an image composed of multiple images. Examples include Gotham's skyline, exterior shots of Wayne Tower, and some of the exterior monorail shots. The climactic monorail sequence mixed live action footage, model work, and CGI.

The bats were entirely digital (except in shots containing only one or two bats), as it was decided directing larger amounts of real bats on set would be problematic. Dead bats were scanned to create digital models. Locations and sets were recreated on the computer so the flying bats would not be superfluous once incorporated into the finished film.

Soundtrack

See also: Batman Begins soundtrack

The score for *Batman Begins* was composed by Hans Zimmer and James Newton Howard. Nolan originally invited Zimmer to compose the music, and Zimmer asked Nolan if he could invite Howard to compose as well, as they had always planned a collaboration. The two composers collaborated on separate themes for the "split personality" of Bruce Wayne and his alter ego, Batman. Zimmer and Howard began composing in Los Angeles and moved to London where they stayed for twelve weeks to complete most of their writing. Zimmer and Howard sought inspiration for shaping the score by visiting the *Batman Begins* sets.

Zimmer wanted to avoid writing music that had been done in earlier Batman films, so the score became an amalgamation of orchestra and electronic music. The film's ninety-piece orchestra was developed from members of various London orchestras, and Zimmer chose to use more than the normal number of cellos. Zimmer enlisted a boy soprano to help reflect the music in some of film's scenes where Bruce Wayne's parents tragic memories are involved. "He's singing a fairly pretty tune and then he gets stuck, it's like froze, arrested development," said Zimmer. He also attempted to add human dimension to Batman, whose behavior would typically be seen as "psychotic", through the music. Both composers collaborated to create 2 hours and 20 minutes worth of music for the film. Zimmer composed the action sequences, while Howard focused on the film's drama.

Themes

Comic book writer and author Danny Fingeroth argues that a strong theme in the film is Bruce's search for a father figure, saying "[Alfred] is the good father that Bruce comes to depend on. Bruce's real father died before they could establish an adult relationship, and Liam Neeson's Ducard is stern and demanding, didactic and challenging, but not a father figure with any sympathy. If Bruce is anyone's son, it is Alfred's. [Morgan] Freeman's Lucius is cool and imperturbable, another steady anchor in Bruce's life." Blogger Mark Fisher states that Bruce's search for justice requires him to learn from a proper father figure, with Thomas Wayne and Ra's al Ghul being the two counterpoints. Alfred provides a maternal figure of unconditional love, despite the overall lack of focus on a mother figure in Bruce's life.

Fingeroth also argues that a major theme in the film is fear, which supports the story of Bruce Wayne becoming a hero. Director Christopher Nolan stated that the idea behind the film was "a person who would confront his innermost fear and then attempt to become it". Fingeroth referred to this film's depiction as "the man with fear—but who rises above it". The theme of fear is further personified by the choice of antagonist, the Scarecrow. The film depicts how fear can affect all creatures regardless of might. Allusions to fear are seen throughout, from Bruce's conquering of his demons, to becoming Batman, to the Scarecrow and his deadly fear toxin. The macabre, distorted images presented in the Scarecrow's toxin-induced hallucinations also express the idea of terror to an extreme.

Critic Brian Orndorf considered *Batman Begins* "fierce" and "demonstrative in brood", giving the film an abundance of gravitas and energy. It strays away from the lighter fare of Joel Schumacher's 1997 Batman film, *Batman & Robin*, which contained camp one-liners throughout. The theme of fear is intensified with the help of the musical score by Zimmer and Howard, which also "eschews traditional heroic themes". Also contrary to previous Batman films, a psychological investigation of Bruce Wayne's split personality in the bat suit is only lightly touched upon. Orndorf noted that Bruce is a "character constantly striving to do the right thing, not worn down by incessant reexamination".

Release

Reception

The film received positive reviews from critics. Based on 257 reviews collected by Rotten Tomatoes, *Batman Begins* currently garners an 84% "fresh" rating. The film's reception was more ambivalent within the 43 reviews in Rotten Tomatoes' "Top Critics" subset, reaching a 60% positive consensus. By comparison, Metacritic calculated an average score of 70 from the 41 reviews it collected.

James Berardinelli applauded Nolan and Goyer's work creating more understanding into "who [Batman] is and what motivates him", something Berardinelli felt Tim Burton's film lacked; at the same time, Berardinelli felt the romantic aspect between Bale and Holmes did not work because the actors lacked the chemistry Christopher Reeve and Margot Kidder (*Superman*), or Tobey Maguire and Kirsten Dunst (*Spider-Man*) shared in their respective roles. According to *Total Film*, Nolan manages to create such strong characters and story that the third-act action sequences cannot compare to " the frisson of two people talking", and Katie Holmes and Christian Bale's romantic subplot has a spark "refreshingly free of Peter Parker/Mary Jane-style whining".

Los Angeles Times' Kenneth Turan, who felt the film began slowly, stated that the "story, psychology and reality, not special effects", assisted the darkness behind Batman's arsenal; he noted that Neeson and Holmes, unlike Bale's ability to "feel his role in his bones", do not appear to fit their respective characters in "being both comic-book archetypes and real people". *The New Yorker*'s David Denby did not share Berardinelli and Turan's opinion. He was unimpressed with the film, when comparing it to the two Tim Burton films, and that Christian Bale's presence was hindered by the "dull earnestness of the screenplay", the final climax was "cheesy and unexciting", and that Nolan had resorted to imitating the "fakery" used by other filmmakers when filming action sequences.

Michael Wilmington of the *Chicago Tribune* believed Nolan and Miller managed to "comfortably mix the tormented drama and revenge motifs with light hearted gags and comic book allusions", and that Nolan takes the series out of the "slam-bang Hollywood jokefests" the franchise had drifted into.

Comic book scribe and editor Dennis O'Neil stated that he "felt the filmmakers really understood the character they were translating", citing this film as the best of the live-action Batman films. In contrast, J.R. Jones, from the *Chicago Reader*, criticized the script, and Nolan and David Goyer for not living up to the "hype about exploring Batman's damaged psyche". Roger Ebert, who gave mixed reviews to the previous films, wrote this was "the Batman movie I've been waiting for; more correctly, this is the movie I did not realize I was waiting for". Giving it four out of four stars, he commended the realistic portrayals of the Batman arsenal — the Batsuit, Batcave, Batmobile, and the Batsignal — as well as the focus on "the story and character" with less stress on "high-tech action".

Like Berardinelli, *USA Today*'s Mike Clark thought Bale performed the role of Batman as well as he did Patrick Bateman in *American Psycho*, but that the relationship between Bruce Wayne and Rachel Dawes was "frustratingly underdeveloped". Kyle Smith thought Bale exhibited "both the menace and the wit he showed in his brilliant turn in *American Psycho*", and that the film works so well because of the realism, stating, "Batman starts stripping away each layer of Gotham crime only to discover a sicker and more monstrous evil beneath, his rancid city simultaneously invokes early '90s New York, when criminals frolicked to the tune of five murders a day; *Serpico* New York, when cops were for sale; and today, when psychos seek to kill us all at once rather than one by one." In contrast, Salon.com's Stephanie Zacharek felt Nolan did not deliver the emotional depth expected of "one of the most soulful and tortured superheroes of all"; she thought Bale, unlike Michael Keaton who she compared him to, failed to connect with the audience underneath the mask, but that Gary Oldman succeeds in "emotional complexity" where the rest of the movie fails. However, Tim Burton felt Nolan "captured the real spirit that these kind of movies are supposed to have nowadays. When I did *Batman* twenty years ago, in 1988 or something, it was a different time in comic book movies. You couldn't go into that dark side of comics yet. The last couple of years that has become acceptable and Nolan certainly got more to the root of what the Batman comics are about."

Box office

Batman Begins opened on June 15, 2005 in the United States and Canada in 3,858 theaters, including 55 IMAX theaters. The film ranked at the top in its opening weekend, accumulating $48,745,440, which was seen as "strong but unimpressive by today's instantaneous blockbuster standards". The film's five-day gross was $72.9 million, beating *Batman Forever* (1995) as the franchise high. *Batman Begins* also broke the five-day opening record in the 55 IMAX theaters, grossing $3.16 million. Polled moviegoers rated the film with an A, and according to the studio's surveys, *Batman Begins* was considered the best of all the *Batman* films. The audience's demographic was 57 percent male and 54 percent people over the age of 25.

The film held its top spot for another weekend, accumulating $27,589,389 in a 43 percent drop from its first weekend. *Batman Begins* went on to gross $205,343,774 domestically and had a worldwide total of $372,710,015. It is the third-highest grossing Batman film to date, behind Tim Burton's *Batman*, which grossed $411,348,924 worldwide and *The Dark Knight* which has grossed over $1 billion. In comparison to the previous Batman films, *Batman Begins* averaged $12,634 per theater. It was released in more theaters, but sold fewer tickets then the other previous Batman movies, with the exception of *Batman & Robin*. *Batman Begins* was the eighth-highest grossing film of 2005 in the US.

Home media

The DVD of *Batman Begins* was released on October 18, 2005 in both single disc and two-disc deluxe editions. In addition to the film, the deluxe edition contained featurettes and other bonus materials. The edition contained a small paperback booklet, the first *Batman* story *Detective Comics* #27, as well as *Batman: The Man Who Falls* and an excerpt from *Batman: The Long Halloween*. *Batman Begins* achieved first place in national sales and rental charts in October 2005, becoming the top-selling DVD in the fourth quarter of 2005. The DVD grossed $11.36 million in rental revenue. The DVD held its position at the top of the sales chart for a second week, but fell to second place behind *Bewitched* on video rental charts.

Batman Begins was released on HD DVD on October 10, 2006. A *Limited Edition Giftset* of the film was released on DVD and Blu-ray on July 8, 2008, to coincide with *The Dark Knight* which hit theaters July 18, 2008. Due to the successful box office performance of *The Dark Knight*, the *Batman Begins* DVD has seen an increase in both sales and rentals. The film grossed $125,000,000 in DVD sales, bringing its total film gross to $496,853,783.

Tie-in products

Three novels, *Dead White*, *Inferno*, and *Fear Itself*, based on the film's version of Batman were released. All of them took place after the events of the film. In addition, a novelization written by Denny O'Neil, and a video game were released.

Accolades

Wally Pfister was nominated for Best Cinematography at the 78th Academy Awards, receiving the film's only Oscar nomination. The film received three nominations at the 59th BAFTA Awards. Just months after its release, *Batman Begins* was voted by *Empire* readers as the 36th greatest film of all time. In 2006, the American Society of Composers, Authors and Publishers honored James Newton Howard, Hans Zimmer, and Ramin Djawadi with an ASCAP award for composing a film that became one of the top grossing films of 2005. The film was awarded three Saturn Awards in 2006 as well: Best Fantasy Film, Best Actor for Christian Bale, and Best Writing for Nolan and Goyer. Christian Bale would go on to win an MTV Movie Award for Best Hero. However, Katie Holmes's performance was not well received, and she was nominated for a Razzie Award for Worst Supporting Actress. *Batman Begins* won the fan-based *Total Film* award for Best Film.

Impact

Shawn Adler of *MTV* stated *Batman Begins* heralded a trend of darker genre films, that either retold back-stories or rebooted them altogether. Examples he cited were *Casino Royale*, as well as the in-development *RoboCop*, *Red Sonja*, and *He-Man*. Filmmakers, screenwriters and producers who have mentioned the film to describe their projects include: Jon Favreau and *Iron Man*, Edward Norton and *The Incredible Hulk*, McG and *Terminator Salvation* (which also stars Bale), Damon Lindelof and *Star Trek*, Robert Downey, Jr. and *Sherlock Holmes*, Lorenzo di Bonaventura and *G.I. Joe: The Rise of Cobra*, and Hugh Jackman and *X-Men Origins: Wolverine*.

External links

- Official website [1]
- *Batman Begins* [2] at the Internet Movie Database
- *Batman Begins* [3] at Allmovie
- *Batman Begins* [4] at Rotten Tomatoes
- *Batman Begins* [6] at Box Office Mojo
- *Batman Begins* [5] hype at Superhero Hype!
- Batman Begins [6] at the Open Directory Project
- Official production notes [7]
- Scene-by-scene annotations of *Batman Begins* [8]
- Comic Vs. Film analysis [9] at IGN
- Film analysis [10] at IGN

Insomnia (2002 film)

Insomnia	
Theatrical release poster	
Directed by	Christopher Nolan
Produced by	Broderick Johnson Paul Junger Witt Andrew A. Kosove Edward L. McDonnell
Written by	Erik Skjoldbjærg Nikolaj Frobenius (1997 screenplay) Hilary Seitz
Starring	Al Pacino Robin Williams Hilary Swank
Music by	David Julyan
Cinematography	Wally Pfister
Editing by	Dody Dorn
Studio	Alcon Entertainment Section Eight
Distributed by	Warner Bros.
Release date(s)	May 24, 2002
Running time	118 minutes
Country	United States
Language	English
Budget	$46 million
Gross revenue	$113,714,830

Insomnia is a 2002 American thriller film directed by Christopher Nolan and stars Al Pacino, Robin Williams, and Hilary Swank. It is a remake of the 1997 film of the same name. The film was released on 24 May 2002.

Plot

In the small fishing town of Nightmute, Alaska, a local 17-year-old girl named Kay Connell (Crystal Lowe) is found murdered. Two LAPD detectives, Will Dormer (Al Pacino) and Hap Eckhart (Martin Donovan) are sent up to assist the local police with their investigation.

Concurrently, an intense Internal Affairs investigation back in Los Angeles is about to put Dormer under the microscope. Dormer is, in fact, guilty of planting false evidence against at least one suspect in this earlier case, a man named Dobbs. Certain that Dobbs was responsible for kidnapping and murdering a young boy, but realizing that there was not enough evidence to support a conviction, Dormer planted forensic evidence in Dobbs' apartment. Dormer fears that many of his legitimate convictions will be overturned if Internal Affairs discovers that he falsified evidence in the Dobbs case. He does not want his life's work destroyed, nor does he want these criminals back on the streets. Early in the movie, Dormer's partner, Eckhart, reveals that Internal Affairs has offered him an immunity deal in exchange for his testimony. Dormer tries to talk Eckhart out of it, but Eckhart, apparently complicit to some degree in Dormer's misdeeds, says that ultimately he must look out for himself and his family first, so he feels he has no choice but to accept the deal.

Focusing now on the Nightmute case, Dormer comes up with a clever plan to lure the murderer back to the scene of the crime. However, the stakeout attempt is blown, and the murder suspect flees into the fog, forcing the police to spread out and search for him on foot. During the pursuit, Dormer sees a figure through the fog, which he believes to be the armed murder suspect. He fires, and the figure collapses. However, when Dormer approaches, he discovers that he has mistakenly shot Eckhart. When Dormer realizes what he's done and tries to help, Eckhart turns away in horror, believing that Dormer shot him to prevent him from testifying in the Internal Affairs investigation. Eckhart dies moments later. As none of the other officers witnessed Eckhart's shooting, it is initially assumed that he was shot by the fleeing murder suspect. Given the nature of Eckhart's impending testimony, Dormer knows that Internal Affairs will never believe that the shooting was accidental. Thus, Dormer faces the dilemma of trying to bring the murder suspect to justice while at the same time cover up the truth about Eckhart's shooting and preserve the misconception that the murder suspect was responsible for that as well. Ellie Burr (Hilary Swank), a young police officer and Dormer's biggest fan, is put in charge of the investigation into Eckhart's shooting.

Throughout the film, Dormer becomes more and more unhinged, partly because of feelings of guilt over shooting his partner and anxiety about the risk of being found out, and partly because of insomnia brought on by the perpetual daylight of the Alaskan summer. Adding to his delirium are the phone calls he receives from Kay's killer, who does not identify himself, but who saw Dormer shoot Eckhart and knows about his attempt to cover it up. Dormer is aware that Kay was a fan of a crime writer named Walter Finch (Robin Williams), and books autographed by him were found among her possessions. He discovers that Finch lives in Alaska, not far from the crime scene, and so starts to suspect Finch is the killer. He finds Finch's address and enters his apartment illegally. There, he finds his photo. Finch returns to his apartment while Dormer is there, realizes Dormer has identified him, and flees. Dormer goes in pursuit, but Finch escapes. Finch contacts Dormer again, and they arrange to meet. Finch offers Dormer a deal, where Dormer is supposed to help frame Kay's abusive boyfriend Randy Stetz (Jonathan Jackson) for the murder in exchange for Finch's silence about the Eckhart shooting. Finch secretly tape records their conversation, in order to give him hard evidence of Dormer's role in the shooting, as well as Dormer's attempt to cover it up. He then lets Dormer know he taped the conversation, a move designed to ensure Dormer's silence. Dormer seemingly agrees to the plan, though he's really just stalling for time. Unfortunately, Finch is impatient and manages to frame Randy all by himself. When Randy is arrested for murder, Dormer is forced to choose between destroying his own reputation and allowing an innocent man to be sent to prison.

Meanwhile, Burr finds some inconsistencies in the Eckhart shooting: she finds a 9mm shell casing at the scene. Reading a case report on one of Dormer's old cases, she learns that Dormer carries a backup gun, a 9mm Walther, now leading her to suspect that Dormer shot his own partner. Later, while meeting with Finch at his cabin, Burr discovers the murder victim's dress. Realizing that Finch is the murderer, she reaches for her gun, but Finch knocks her unconscious. Dormer races to the cabin to confront Finch. It is clear that his concentration is nearly gone due to his lack of sleep. A brief fight ensues between Dormer and Finch, before a now conscious Burr arrives and Finch escapes to his shed. Burr holds Dormer at gunpoint, revealing that she knows he shot Eckhart and demands to know whether he did it on purpose. Dormer breaks down, admitting that he shot his partner and stating that he is no longer certain whether it was an accident or not. From the protection of his shed, Finch fires at them with his shotgun. While Burr and Finch trade gunshots, Dormer sneaks around to Finch's location. Finch fatally wounds Dormer with Burr's original weapon, but Dormer quickly picks up the shotgun and blasts Finch at point blank in the stomach. A stunned Finch dies and tumbles into the water.

Burr rushes to the detective's aid. She comforts Dormer by affirming that Eckhart's shooting was accidental, and tries to toss the evidence—the 9mm shell casing—found from the scene. Dormer stops Burr, telling her not to lose her way. "Let me sleep," asks Dormer—whose name echoes the Latin verb *dormire*, "to sleep", as well as the English words derived from it—before finally dying. After a moment of contemplation, Burr slips the shell casing back into its plastic evidence bag.

Cast

- Al Pacino as Detective Will Dormer
- Robin Williams as Walter Finch
- Hilary Swank as Ellie Burr
- Martin Donovan as Detective Hap Eckhart
- Maura Tierney as Rachel Clement
- Paul Dooley as Chief Nyback
- Jay Brazeau as Francis

- Nicky Katt as Fred Duggar
- Larry Holden as Farrell
- Lorne Cardinal as Rich
- Katharine Isabelle as Tanya Francke
- Jonathan Jackson as Randy Stetz
- Crystal Lowe as Kay Connell

Reception

Critics' reviews were extremely positive, with a "Certified Fresh" rating of 92% on Rotten Tomatoes. The website reported the critical consensus, "Driven by Pacino's performance, Insomnia is a smart and riveting psychological drama."

Novelization

Robert Westbrook adapted the screenplay to novel form, which was published by Onyx in May 2002.

External links

- Official website [1]
- *Insomnia* [2] at the Internet Movie Database
- *Insomnia* [3] at Allmovie
- *Insomnia* [5] at Box Office Mojo
- *Insomnia* [4] at Rotten Tomatoes
- Peter Cowie essay on the original at Criterion.com [5]
- Insomnia Screenshot Gallery at NolanFans [6]

Following

Following	
Directed by	Christopher Nolan
Produced by	Emma Thomas Jeremy Theobald Peter Broderick
Written by	Christopher Nolan
Starring	Jeremy Theobald Alex Haw Lucy Russell John Nolan
Music by	David Julyan
Cinematography	Christopher Nolan
Editing by	Gareth Heal Christopher Nolan
Studio	Syncopy Films Next Wave Films
Distributed by	Zeitgeist Films (US) Momentum Pictures (UK)
Release date(s)	12 September 1998 (Toronto International Film Festival) 2 April 1999 (New York City) 5 November 1999 (UK)
Running time	69 min.
Country	United Kingdom
Language	English
Budget	$6,000
Gross revenue	$48,482

Following is a 1998 neo-noir film directed by Christopher Nolan. It tells the story of a young man who follows strangers around the streets of London and is drawn into a criminal underworld when he fails to keep his distance. The film was made on a small budget and features an unusual non-linear plot structure which has been a structure in several of Christopher Nolan's films.

Plot

A struggling, unemployed young writer takes to following strangers around the streets of London, ostensibly to find inspiration for his first novel.

Initially, he sets strict rules for himself regarding whom he should follow and for how long, but soon discards them as he focuses on a well-groomed man in a dark suit. The man in the suit, having noticed he is being followed, quickly confronts the young man and introduces himself as "Cobb". Cobb reveals that he is a serial burglar and invites the young man to accompany him on various burglaries. The material gains from these crimes seem to be of secondary importance to Cobb, who takes pleasure in rifling through the personal items in his targets' flats, such as drinking their wine. He explains that his true passion is using the shock of robbery and violation of property to make his victims re-examine their lives. He sums up his attitude thus: "You take it away, and show them what they had."

The young man is thrilled by Cobb's lifestyle. He attempts break-ins of his own, as Cobb encourages and guides him. At Cobb's suggestion, he alters his appearance, cutting his hair short and wearing a dark suit. The young man assumes the name of Daniel Lloyd based on the credit card Cobb gives to him and the young man begins to pursue a relationship with a blonde woman whom he meets at a bar and who claims to be the girlfriend of a local gangster. It is later revealed that he and Cobb had broken into her flat prior to this first meeting. Soon, the blonde confides that the gangster is blackmailing her with incriminating photographs. The young man breaks into the gangster's safe, but the only photos he finds are innocuous modelling shots. After confronting the blonde, he learns that she and Cobb have been manipulating him into mimicking Cobb's methods to frame him for Cobb's recent murder charge.

The young man leaves to turn himself in to the police. The blonde reports her success to Cobb, who then reveals that he actually works for the gangster and has a plan of his own. In order to stop the blonde from blackmailing the gangster with evidence from a recent murder, Cobb kills her. Once the young man finishes his story to the police, he learns that he has been framed for the blonde's murder, which was Cobb's plan for him all along. As the young man is arrested, Cobb disappears into a crowd.

Cast

- Jeremy Theobald as The Young Man
- Alex Haw as Cobb
- Lucy Russell as The Blonde
- John Nolan as The Policeman
- Dick Bradsell as The Bald Guy
- Gillian El-Kadi as Home Owner
- Jennifer Angel as Waitress
- Nicolas Carlotti as Barman
- Darren Ormandy as Accountant

- Guy Greenway as Heavy #1
- Tassos Stevens as Heavy #2
- Tristan Martin as Man at Bar
- Rebecca James as Woman at Bar
- Paul Mason as Home Owner's Friend
- David Bovill as Home Owner's Husband

Production

Following was written, directed, filmed, and co-produced by Christopher Nolan. It was filmed in London, England, on black-and-white 16mm film stock. Nolan used a non-linear plot structure for his movie, a device he again used in *Memento*, *Batman Begins* and *The Prestige*. This type of storytelling, he says, reflected the audience's inherent uncertainty about characters in film noir:

> In a compelling story of this genre we are continually being asked to rethink our assessment of the relationship between the various characters, and I decided to structure my story in such a way as to emphasize the audience's incomplete understanding of each new scene as it is first presented.

Following was written and planned to be as inexpensive to produce as possible, but Nolan has described the production of *Following* as "extreme", even for a low-budget shoot. With little money, limited equipment, and a cast and crew who were all in full-time employment on weekdays, the shoot took a full year to complete.

To conserve expensive film stock, every scene in the film was rehearsed extensively to ensure that the first or second take could be used in the final edit. For the most part, Nolan filmed without professional film lighting equipment, employing only available light. He also used the homes of his friends and family as locations.

Reception

Following received generally positive reviews. Its aggregate review score from Rottentomatoes.com is 76%.

Los Angeles Times reviewer Kevin Thomas was particularly impressed with the film, saying that it was a "taut and ingenious neo-noir" and that "as a psychological mystery it plays persuasively if not profoundly. Nolan relishes the sheer nastiness he keeps stirred up, unabated for 70 minutes." *TV Guide* called it "short, sharp and tough as nails", praising its fast-paced storytelling and 'tricky, triple-tiered flashback structure'. David Thompson of *Sight and Sound* commented that "Nolan shows a natural talent for a fluent handheld aesthetic."

However, Tony Rayns felt that the film's climax was uninspired, saying that "the generic pay off is a little disappointing after the edgy, character based scenes of exposition". *Empire*'s Trevor Lewis questioned the skill of the film's inexperienced cast, saying that they "lack the dramatic ballast to compensate for [Nolan's] erratic plot elisions." In contrast, David Thompson was of the opinion that the "unfamiliar cast acquit themselves well in a simple naturalistic style."

External links

- *Following* [1] at the Internet Movie Database
- *Following* [2] at Allmovie
- *Following* [3] at Rotten Tomatoes
- Following [4], Matinee Idles Podcast

The Prestige (film)

The Prestige	
Promotional poster	
Directed by	Christopher Nolan
Produced by	• Christopher Nolan • Emma Thomas
Written by	• Jonathan Nolan • Christopher Nolan • Christopher Priest (novel)
Starring	• Hugh Jackman • Christian Bale • Michael Caine • Scarlett Johansson • David Bowie • Piper Perabo • Andy Serkis • Rebecca Hall
Music by	David Julyan
Cinematography	Wally Pfister
Editing by	Lee Smith
Studio	• Newmarket Films • Syncopy Films
Distributed by	Touchstone Pictures Warner Bros.
Release date(s)	October 20, 2006
Running time	130 minutes
Country	United States
Language	English
Budget	$40 million
Gross revenue	$109,676,311

The Prestige is a 2006 mystery thriller film directed by Christopher Nolan, with a screenplay adapted from Christopher Priest's 1995 novel of the same name. The story follows Robert Angier and Alfred Borden, rival stage magicians in London at the end of the 19th century. Obsessed with creating the best stage illusion, they engage in competitive one-upmanship with tragic results.

The film features Hugh Jackman as Robert Angier, Christian Bale as Alfred Borden, and David Bowie as Nikola Tesla. It also stars Michael Caine, Scarlett Johansson, Piper Perabo, Andy Serkis, and Rebecca Hall. The film reunites Nolan with actors Bale and Caine from *Batman Begins*, and returning cinematographer Wally Pfister, production designer Nathan Crowley, film score composer David Julyan, and editor Lee Smith.

Priest's epistolary novel was adapted to the screen by Nolan and his brother, Jonathan Nolan, using Nolan's distinctive nonlinear narrative structure. Themes of duality, obsession, sacrifice, and secrecy pervade the conflict. The film was released on October 20, 2006, receiving good reviews and strong box office results, and obtained Academy Award nominations for Best Cinematography and Best Art Direction.

Plot

Robert Angier and Alfred Borden are plants for Milton the Magician, with Cutter (Caine) as his illusion engineer. Angier's wife drowns while performing a predicament escape from a Chinese water torture cell, and Angier suspects that Borden bound her wrists with a new knot that he had suggested to Cutter before—one harder for her to undo than his customary one. At the funeral, Borden enrages Angier by saying he does not know which knot he tied.

The two men begin separate careers as magicians; Borden becomes "The Professor" and hires an engineer named Bernard Fallon, while Angier performs as "The Great Danton" with Cutter and Olivia as his assistants. During a parlor magic job, Borden meets Sarah; they marry and have a daughter, Jess. Sarah feels uneasy about Borden and his apparent fickleness; she claims to know when he loves her "more than the magic" and when he does not. During Borden's performance of the bullet catch, a disguised Angier again demands to know which knot Borden used. Borden and Fallon quickly realize Angier is going to shoot at Borden with a loaded gun. At the last second, Fallon intervenes, and the bullet severs two of Borden's fingers instead of killing him. A disguised Borden later sabotages Angier's performance of the vanishing bird cage illusion, damaging Angier's reputation.

Borden soon astonishes crowds with "The Transported Man", in which he bounces a ball across the stage before stepping through a door and instantly reappearing from a second door on the opposite side of the stage to catch the ball. The new illusion amazes Angier and Olivia. Obsessed with beating Borden, Angier hires a double and steals Borden's trick, with a slight variation, as "The New Transported Man". The double enjoys the applause while Angier can only listen from below stage. Unhappy at missing the applause and obsessed with figuring out Borden's version of the teleportation illusion, Angier sends Olivia to steal Borden's secrets. Although Olivia provides Angier with Borden's enciphered diary, she falls in love with Borden and double-crosses Angier, allowing Borden to sabotage Angier's act, permanently crippling Angier's left leg by removing a crash mat. In return, Angier and Cutter capture Fallon and bury him alive inside a coffin, revealing his location to Borden in exchange for the key to Borden's illusion. Before rushing to dig out Fallon while he still has air, Borden gives Angier one word, "TESLA", and suggests that it is not merely the key to the transposition cipher of Borden's notebook (which Olivia had brought to Angier) but also the key to the illusion.

Angier travels to Colorado Springs to meet Nikola Tesla and learn the secret of Borden's illusion. Tesla constructs a teleportation machine that resembles a Magnifying Transmitter, but the device initially fails to work. Angier learns from Borden's notebook that he has been sent on a wild goose chase. Feeling he has been cheated, he returns to Tesla's lab, but discovers that the machine creates a duplicate of any item placed in it, which appears some distance away. Tesla is forced to leave Colorado Springs after his rival, Thomas Edison, sends henchmen to torch Tesla's lab, but he leaves Angier an improved version of the machine. In a letter, however, he warns Angier to destroy it.

Borden's relationship with Olivia takes a heavy emotional toll on Sarah, driving her to drink. Borden's erratic behavior and inconsistent affection, along with Sarah's suspicion of an extramarital relationship between Borden and Olivia, leads Sarah to hang herself in Borden's magic workshop. Angier returns to London to produce a final set of 100 performances of his new act, "The Real Transported Man". He insists that Cutter remain front stage for these shows and that only blind stagehands help backstage. In the new illusion, Angier disappears under huge arcs of electricity and instantaneously "teleports" 50 yards from the stage to the balcony. Borden is baffled but spots a trap door. After a show one night, Fallon follows Angier's stagehands. They move a large, concealed water tank across town to an abandoned building. Borden attends Angier's performance again. He slips backstage and discovers a locked water tank with Angier drowning inside. Borden tries to save him, but Angier drowns. Cutter catches Borden, who is convicted of murder and sentenced to hang.

In prison, Borden reads Angier's diary from Colorado which addresses him directly with hopes he will rot in prison for his murder. More troubling to him, his daughter Jess will become a ward of court, unless he accepts a mysterious offer. A man named Lord Caldlow sends his attorney to meet Borden in prison. An avid collector of illusionist paraphernalia, Caldlow asks for all of Borden's secrets and devices, including the truth of "The Transported Man". In exchange, he will adopt Jess, and raise her in a rich and comfortable lifestyle. Borden ultimately agrees to the arrangement, but refuses to reveal all unless he can see her before his execution. When Lord Caldlow visits Borden in person on the day of his hanging, with Jess in tow, Borden realizes that he is Angier. Beaten, Borden gives him a note containing the secret of the original Transported Man trick, but Angier tears it up without reading it. Cutter also meets the lord and realizes he is Angier and that Borden was innocent. Cutter then grasps the full grim cost of Angier's obsession when he sees he has adopted Jess. Cutter is furious that he was the one who indirectly framed Borden, who is subsequently hanged.

Cutter accompanies Angier to the abandoned building where the water tanks are stored, and helps him store the teleportation machine. Cutter leaves in disgust, silently acknowledging the arrival of Borden, who shoots Angier. Borden reveals that he and "Fallon" were identical twins who lived as a single individual, alternating lives as needed. One twin was the husband of Sarah and father to daughter Jess.

The other was in love with Olivia, and it is he who dies in the gallows. For the original illusion, a twin acted as the double. They were so committed to the illusion that they amputated the other twin's fingers to match his brother's injury. Similarly, flashbacks recount Angier's method: that each time he disappeared during his illusion, the machine would create a duplicate, with the first Angier falling through a trap door into a locked tank and drowning, and the duplicate teleporting to the balcony. Each tank stores a drowned duplicate of Angier for each time that he has performed the trick. Before leaving, Alfred Borden looks back at the aisles of tanks containing the dead duplicates and then leaves the dead Angier as a fire begins to consume the building. Afterwards, Cutter reunites Borden with his daughter.

Cast

- Christian Bale as Alfred Borden / The Professor, a working-class magician with an understanding of magic. Christian Bale expressed interest in playing the part of Alfred Borden, and was cast after Jackman. Although Nolan had previously cast Bale as Batman in *Batman Begins*, he did not consider Bale for the part of Borden until Bale contacted him about the script. Nolan said that Bale was "exactly right" for the part of Borden, and that it was "unthinkable" for anyone else to play the part. Nolan described Bale as "terrific to work with", who "takes what he does very, very seriously". Nolan suggested that the actors should not read the book, but Bale ignored his advice.

- Hugh Jackman as Robert Angier / The Great Danton, an aristocratic magician with a talent for performance. After reading the script, Jackman expressed interest in playing the part of Robert Angier. Christopher Nolan discovered Jackman was interested in the script, and after meeting with him, saw that Jackman possessed the qualities of stage showmanship that Nolan was looking for in the role of Angier. Nolan explained that Angier had "a wonderful understanding of the interaction between a performer and a live audience", a quality he believed that Jackman had. Nolan said that "[Jackman] has the great depth as an actor that hasn't really been explored. People haven't had the chance to really see what he can do as an actor, and this is a character that would let him do that." Jackman based his portrayal of Angier on 1950s-era American magician Channing Pollock.

- Michael Caine as John Cutter, the stage engineer who works for Angier. Caine had previously collaborated with Nolan and Bale in *Batman Begins*, where he played Alfred Pennyworth, the Wayne family butler. Nolan said that even though it felt like the character of Cutter was written for Caine, it was not. Nolan noted that the character "was written before I'd ever met him". Caine describes Cutter as "a teacher, a father and a guide to Angier". Caine, in trying to create Cutter's nuanced portrait, altered his voice and posture. Nolan later said that "Michael Caine's character really becomes something of the heart of the movie. He has a wonderful warmth and emotion to him that draws you into the story and allows you to have a point of view on these characters without judging them too harshly."

- Rebecca Hall as Sarah Borden: Borden's wife. Hall had to relocate from North London to Los Angeles in order to shoot the film, though the film itself takes place in North London. Hall said that she "was starstruck just to be involved in [the film]".

- Scarlett Johansson as Olivia Wenscombe, Angier's assistant and Borden's lover. Nolan said that he was "very keen" for Johansson to portray the role, and when he met with her to discuss it, "she just loved the character". Johansson praised Nolan's directing methods, saying that she "loved working with [him]"; he was "incredibly focused and driven and involved, and really involved in the performance in every aspect."

- David Bowie as Nikola Tesla, the real life inventor who creates a device for Angier. For the role of Nikola Tesla, Nolan wanted someone who was not necessarily a film star, but was "extraordinarily charismatic". Nolan said that "David Bowie was really the only guy I had in mind to play Tesla because his function in the story is a small but very important role". Nolan contacted David Bowie, who initially turned down the part. As a lifelong fan of his music, Nolan flew out to New York to pitch the role to Bowie in person, telling him that nobody else could possibly play the part; Bowie accepted after a few minutes.

- Piper Perabo as Julia McCullough, Angier's wife.

- Roger Rees as Owens.

- Andy Serkis as Mr. Alley, Tesla's assistant. Serkis said that he played his character with the belief that he was "once a corporation man who got excited by this maverick, Tesla, so jumped ship and went with the maverick". Serkis described his character as a "gatekeeper", a "conman", and "a mirror image of Michael Caine's character". Serkis, a big fan of Bowie, said that he was enjoyable to work with, describing him as "very unassuming, very down to earth... very at ease with himself and funny."

- Ricky Jay as "Milton the Magician", an older magician Borden and Angier work for at the beginning of the story. Jay, a noted American stage magician, and Michael Weber trained Jackman and Bale for their roles with brief instruction in various stage illusions. The magicians gave the actors limited information, allowing them to know enough to pull off a scene.

Production

Julian Jarrold's and Sam Mendes's producer approached Christopher Priest for an adaptation of his novel *The Prestige*. Priest was impressed with Nolan's films *Following* and *Memento*, and subsequently, producer Valerie Dean brought the book to Christopher Nolan's attention. In October 2000, Christopher Nolan traveled to the UK to publicize *Memento*, as Newmarket Films was having difficulty finding a U.S. distributor. While in London, Christopher Nolan read Priest's book and shared the story with his brother while walking around in Highgate (a location later featured in the scene where Angier ransoms Borden's ingénieur in Highgate Cemetery). The development process for *The Prestige* began as a reversal of their earlier collaboration: Jonathan Nolan had pitched his initial story for *Memento* to his brother during a road trip.

A year later, the option on the book became available and was purchased by Aaron Ryder of Newmarket Films. In late 2001, Christopher Nolan became busy with the post-production of *Insomnia*, and asked Jonathan Nolan to help work on the script. The writing process was a long collaboration between the Nolan brothers, occurring intermittently over a period of five years. In the script, the Nolans emphasized the magic of the story through the dramatic narrative, playing down the visual depiction of stage magic. The three-act screenplay was deliberately structured around the three elements of the film's illusion: the pledge, the turn, and the prestige. "It took a long time to figure out how to achieve cinematic versions of the very literary devices that drive the intrigue of the story," Christopher Nolan told *Variety*. "The shifting points of view, the idea of journals within journals and stories within stories. Finding the cinematic equivalents of those literary devices was very complex." Although the film is thematically faithful to the novel, two major changes were made to the plot structure during the adaptation process: the novel's spiritualism subplot was removed, and the modern-day frame story was replaced with Borden's wait for the gallows. Priest approved of the adaptation, describing it as "an extraordinary and brilliant script, a fascinating adaptation of my novel".

In early 2003, Nolan planned to direct the film before the production of *Batman Begins* accelerated. Following the release of *Batman Begins*, Nolan started up the project again, negotiating with Bale and Jackman in October 2005. While the screenplay was still being written, production designer Nathan Crowley began the set design process in Nolan's garage, employing a "visual script" consisting of scale models, images, drawings, and notes. Jonathan and Christopher Nolan finished the final shooting draft on January 13, 2006, and began production three days later on January 16. Filming ended on April 9.

The historic Tower Theatre in Los Angeles was used as the location for the Pantage Theatre in London

Crowley and his crew searched Los Angeles for almost seventy locations that would resemble fin de siècle London. Jonathan Nolan visited Colorado Springs to research Nikola Tesla and based the electric bulb scene on actual experiments conducted by Tesla. Nathan Crowley helped design the scene for Tesla's invention; It was shot in the parking lot of the Mount Wilson Observatory. Influenced by a "Victorian modernist aesthetic", Crowley chose four locations in the Broadway theater district in downtown Los Angeles for the film's stage magic performances: the Los Angeles Theatre, the Palace Theatre, the Los Angeles Belasco, and the Tower Theatre. Crowley also turned a portion of the Universal back lot into Victorian London. Nolan built only one set for the film, an "under-the-stage section that houses the machinery that makes the larger illusions work," preferring to simply dress various Los Angeles locations and sound stages to stand in for Colorado and Victorian England. In

contrast to most period pieces, Nolan kept up the quick pace of production by shooting with handheld cameras, and refrained from using artificial lighting in some scenes, relying instead on natural light on location. Costume designer Joan Bergin chose attractive, modern Victorian fashions for Scarlett Johansson; cinematographer Wally Pfister captured the mood with soft earth tones as white and black colors provided background contrasts, bringing actors' faces to the foreground.

Editing, scoring and mixing finished on September 22, 2006. The song "Analyse" by Radiohead frontman Thom Yorke is played over the credits.

Themes

See also: Nikola Tesla in popular culture

The rivalry between Borden and Angier dominates the film. Obsession, secrecy, and sacrifice fuel the battle, as both magicians contribute their fair share to a deadly duel of one-upmanship, with disastrous results. Angier's obsession with beating Borden costs him Cutter's friendship, while Borden's obsession with maintaining the secrecy of his twin leads Sarah to question their relationship, eventually resulting in her suicide; in the end, Angier and Borden both lose Olivia's love because of their obsessions. Their struggle is also expressed through class warfare: Borden as The Professor, a working-class magician who gets his hands dirty, versus Angier as The Great Danton, a classy showman whose accent makes him appear American. Film critic Matt Brunson observes a complex theme of duality exemplified by Angier and Borden, noting that the film dispenses with simplistic notions of good versus evil characters.

Angier's theft of Borden's teleportation illusion in the film echoes the many real-world examples of stolen tricks among magicians. Outside the film, similar rivalries include magicians John Nevil Maskelyne and Harry Kellar's dispute over a levitation illusion. Gary Westfahl of *Locus Online* also notes a "new proclivity for mayhem" in the film over the novel, citing the murder/suicide disposition of Angier's duplicates and intensified violent acts of revenge and counter-revenge. This "relates to a more general alteration in the events and tone of the film" rather than significantly changing the underlying themes.

Nor is this cutthroat competition limited to prestidigitation: engineering "wizards" Nikola Tesla and Thomas Edison engaged in a rivalry over electrical current, which appears in the film in parallel to Borden and Angier's competition for magical supremacy.

Den Shewman of *Creative Screenwriting* says the film asks how far one would go to devote oneself to an art. The character of Chung Ling Soo, according to Shewman, is a metaphor for this theme. Film critic Alex Manugian refers to this theme as the "meaning of commitment." For example, Soo's pretense of being slow and feeble misdirects his audience from noticing the physical strength required to perform the goldfish bowl trick, but the cost of maintaining this illusion is the sacrifice of individuality: Soo's true appearance and freedom to act naturally are consciously suppressed in his ceaseless dedication to the art of magic.

Nicolas Rapold of *Film Comment* addresses the points raised by Shewman and Manugian in terms of the film's "refracted take on Romanticism":

> Angier's technological solution – which suggests art as sacrifice, a phoenix-like death of the self - and Borden's more meat-and-potatoes form of stagecraft embody the divide between the artist and the social being.

For Manugian the central theme is "obsession," but he also notes the supporting themes of the "nature of deceit" and "science as magic." Manugian criticizes the Nolans for trying to "ram too many themes into the story."

Music

English musician and film score composer David Julyan penned the music for *The Prestige*. Julyan had previously collaborated with director Christopher Nolan on *Memento* and *Insomnia*. Like the film, the soundtrack was divided into three sections: the Pledge, the Turn, and the Prestige.

Some critics were disappointed with the score, acknowledging that while it worked within the context of the film, it was not enjoyable by itself. Jonathan Jarry of SoundtrackNet described the score as "merely functional", establishing the atmosphere of dread but never taking over. Although the reviewer was interested with the score's notion, Jarry found the execution was "extremely disappointing".

Christopher Coleman of Tracksounds felt that although it was "a perfectly fitting score", it was completely overwhelmed by the film itself, and was totally unnoticed at times. Christian Clemmensen of Filmtracks recommended the soundtrack for those who enjoyed Julyan's work on the film, and noted that it was not for those who expected "any semblance of intellect or enchantment in the score to match the story of the film." Clemmensen called the score lifeless, "constructed on a bed of simplistic string chords and dull electronic soundscapes."

Reception

Touchstone opted to move the release date up a week, from the original October 27, to October 20, 2006. The film earned $14,801,808 on opening weekend in the United States, debuting at #1. It proceeded to gross $109 million, of which $53 million was from the US. The film received nominations for the Academy Award for Best Art Direction and the Academy Award for Best Cinematography, as well as a nomination for the Hugo Award for Best Dramatic Presentation, Long Form in 2007.

The Prestige received generally favorable reviews from film critics,. *Rotten Tomatoes* reported that 75% of critics gave the film positive reviews, with an average score of 7.1/10, based upon a sample of 179 reviews. At *Metacritic*, which assigns a normalized rating out of 100 to reviews from mainstream critics, the film received an average score of 66, based on 36 reviews. Claudia Puig of *USA Today* described the film as "one of the most innovative, twisting, turning art films of the past decade." Drew

McWeeny gave the film a glowing review, saying it demands repeat viewing, with Peter Travers of *Rolling Stone* agreeing. Richard Roeper and guest critic A.O. Scott gave the film a "two thumbs up" rating. Todd Gilchrist of IGN applauded the performances of Bale and Jackman whilst praising Nolan for making "this complex story as easily understandable and effective as he made the outwardly straightforward comic book adaptation (*Batman Begins*) dense and sophisticated... any truly great performance is almost as much showmanship as it is actual talent, and Nolan possesses both in spades." *CNN.com* and *Village Voice* film critic Tom Charity listed it amongst his best films of 2006. Philip French of *The Observer* recommended the film, comparing the rivalry between the two main characters to that of Mozart and Salieri in the highly acclaimed *Amadeus*.

On the other hand, Dennis Harvey of *Variety* criticized the film as gimmicky, though he felt the cast did well in underwritten roles. Kirk Honeycutt of *The Hollywood Reporter* felt that characters "are little more than sketches. Remove their obsessions, and the two magicians have little personality". Nonetheless, the two reviewers praised David Bowie as Tesla, as well as the production values and cinematography. On a simpler note, Emanuel Levy has said: "Whether viewers perceive *The Prestige* as intricately complex or just unnecessarily complicated would depend to a large degree on their willingness to suspend disbelief for two hours." He gave the film a B grade.

Roger Ebert gave the film three stars out of four, he described the revelation at the end a "fundamental flaw" and a "cheat". He wrote, "The pledge of Nolan's *The Prestige* is that the film, having been metaphorically sawed in two, will be restored; it fails when it cheats, as, for example, if the whole woman produced on the stage were not the same one so unfortunately cut in two." R.J. Carter of *The Trades* felt, "I love a good science fiction story; just tell me in advance." He gave the film a B-. Author Christopher Priest saw the film three times as of January 5, 2007, and his reaction was "'Well, holy shit.' I was thinking, 'God, I like that,' and 'Oh, I wish I'd thought of that.'"

Blu-ray and DVD release

The Region 1 disc is by Buena Vista Home Entertainment, and was released on February 20, 2007, and is available on DVD and BD formats. The Warner Bros. Region 2 DVD was released on March 12, 2007. It is also available in both BD and regionless HD DVD in Europe (before HD DVD was canceled). Special features are minimal, with the documentary *Director's Notebook: The Prestige – Five Making-of Featurettes*, running roughly twenty minutes combined, an art gallery and the trailer. Nolan did not contribute to a commentary as he felt the film primarily relied on an audience's reaction and did not want to remove the mystery from the story.

External links

- Official website [1]
- *The Prestige* [2] at the Internet Movie Database
- *The Prestige* [7] at Box Office Mojo
- *The Prestige* [3] at Allmovie
- *The Prestige* [4] at Rotten Tomatoes

The Dark Knight (film)

The Dark Knight	
Theatrical release poster	
Directed by	Christopher Nolan
Produced by	Christopher Nolan Charles Roven Emma Thomas
Screenplay by	Christopher Nolan Jonathan Nolan
Story by	David S. Goyer Christopher Nolan *Comic book*: Bob Kane Bill Finger
Starring	Christian Bale Michael Caine Heath Ledger Gary Oldman Aaron Eckhart Maggie Gyllenhaal Morgan Freeman
Music by	Hans Zimmer James Newton Howard
Cinematography	Wally Pfister
Editing by	Lee Smith
Studio	Legendary Pictures Syncopy Films
Distributed by	Warner Bros.
Release date(s)	July 14, 2008 (New York City) July 18, 2008
Running time	152 minutes
Country	United States
Language	English
Budget	$185 million

Gross revenue	$1,001,921,825
Preceded by	*Batman Begins*

The Dark Knight is a 2008 superhero film directed and co-written by Christopher Nolan. Based on the DC Comics character Batman, the film is part of Nolan's *Batman* film series and a sequel to 2005's *Batman Begins*. Christian Bale reprises the lead role. The film follows Bruce Wayne/Batman (Bale), District Attorney Harvey Dent (Aaron Eckhart), Assistant D.A. Rachel Dawes (Maggie Gyllenhaal), and Police Commissioner James Gordon (Gary Oldman) and their struggles and journey in combating the new rising threat of a criminal who goes by the name of the "Joker" (Heath Ledger).

Nolan's inspiration for the film was the Joker's comic book debut in 1940, and the 1996 series *The Long Halloween*, which retold Two-Face's origin. *The Dark Knight* was filmed primarily in Chicago, as well as in several other locations in the United States, the United Kingdom, and Hong Kong. Nolan used an IMAX camera to film some sequences, including the Joker's first appearance in the film.

On January 22, 2008, after he had completed filming *The Dark Knight*, Heath Ledger died from a toxic combination of prescription drugs, leading to intense attention from the press and moviegoing public. Warner Bros. had initially created a viral marketing campaign for *The Dark Knight*, developing promotional websites and trailers highlighting screen shots of Ledger as the Joker, but after Ledger's death, the studio refocused its promotional campaign.

The Dark Knight was released on July 16, 2008 in Australia, on July 18, 2008 in North America, and on July 24, 2008 in the United Kingdom. Critically acclaimed, it set numerous records during its theatrical run and is currently one of only three films to have earned more than $500 million at the North American box office. With over $1 billion in revenue worldwide, it is the seventh highest-grossing film of all time (unadjusted for inflation). The film received eight Academy Award nominations and won for Best Sound Editing and Best Supporting Actor for Ledger's performance.

Plot

In Gotham City, the Joker and his accomplices rob a mob bank. Batman and Lieutenant James Gordon decide to include new district attorney Harvey Dent, who is dating Rachel Dawes, in their plan to eradicate the mob. Bruce later meets Harvey and offers him a fundraiser after realizing his sincerity. Mob bosses Sal Maroni, Gambol, and the Chechen meet with other criminals to discuss the new pressure on their crime operations. Lau, a Chinese mafia accountant, informs them that he has hidden their money and fled to Hong Kong in an attempt to preempt Gordon's plan to seize their funds and hide from Dent's jurisdiction. The Joker appears, warning that Batman will come after Lau, and instead offers to kill Batman for half of the funds. They flatly refuse and Gambol places a bounty on the Joker's head. Not long after, the Joker kills Gambol and takes control of his men.

In Hong Kong, Batman captures Lau with a skyhook and delivers him to the Gotham City police where Lau agrees to testify, letting Dent and Gordon arrest the mob. In retaliation the Joker issues an ultimatum to Gotham that people will die each day unless Batman reveals his identity, resulting in the deaths of Commissioner Gillian B. Loeb and the judge presiding over the mob trials. Gordon foils Joker's assassination attempt on the mayor and is apparently killed. As a result, Bruce plans to reveal his persona, but Harvey instead reveals himself as Batman to protect the truth and is taken into protective custody. Escorted across the city, Harvey is pursued by the Joker while Batman rushes to aid. Gordon, who faked his death to lure the Joker, arrests him with Batman's help and is promoted to Commissioner. However, Harvey goes missing and the Joker reveals that he, along with Rachel, have been taken to separate buildings on opposite sides of town which will explode at the same time. Batman goes after Rachel whilst Gordon and the police go for Harvey. At the same time the Joker escapes custody with Lau using a smuggled bomb. Batman instead finds Harvey and rescues him though he pressures him to go for Rachel. The buildings explode; Rachel dies while half of Harvey's face is burnt in his escape, leaving him traumatized and vengeful.

After killing Lau and the Chechen, the Joker threatens to destroy a hospital if Coleman Reese, an accountant at Wayne Enterprises who discovers Batman's identity, is not dead within an hour. Bruce saves Reese, whilst the Joker visits Harvey in the hospital and convinces him to go on a personal vendetta against those who played a part in Rachel's death. Now Two-Face, Harvey judges Joker by the toss of a coin and spares him. The Joker blows up the hospital and leaves with a bus of hostages, whilst Two-Face confronts and kills Maroni and others. That night, as civilians are evacuated from the city, the Joker has two ferries rigged with explosives, offering both civilian and prisoner passenger groups to destroy the other ferry to live. Batman stops Gordon's SWAT teams from taking out the Joker, in order to protect the hostages and to capture the Joker himself. The ferry passengers refuse to kill one another and the Joker is captured, but not before explaining his complex relationship with Batman and revealing what he has done to Harvey; stating that while Batman is truly incorruptible, Harvey was not.

At the remains of the building where Rachel died, Batman finds Two-Face holding Gordon and his family at gunpoint. Two-Face judges the fate of Batman, himself, and Gordon's son with three coin tosses. As the result of the first two flips, he shoots Batman in the abdomen and spares himself. Flipping the coin to determine the boy's fate, Two-Face is tackled over the side by a wounded Batman, resulting in Two-Face's death. Knowing that the citizens of Gotham will lose hope and all morale if Harvey's rampage becomes known, Gordon is convinced by Batman to hold Batman publicly responsible for the murders. The police swarm the building, and a manhunt for Batman ensues. Gordon later delivers the eulogy at Harvey's funeral and smashes the Bat-Signal.

Cast

- Christian Bale as Bruce Wayne / Batman, a billionaire dedicated to protecting Gotham City from the criminal underworld by night. Bale said he was confident in his choice to return in the role because of the positive response to his portrayal in *Batman Begins*. He continued training in the Keysi Fighting Method and performed many of his own stunts, but did not gain as much muscle as in the previous film because the new Batsuit allowed him to move with greater agility. Bale described Batman's dilemma as whether "[his crusade is] something that has an end. Can he quit and have an ordinary life? The kind of manic intensity someone has to have to maintain the passion and the anger that they felt as a child, takes an effort after a while, to keep doing that. At some point, you

Cast and crew of *The Dark Knight* at the European premiere in London. From left to right: Director Christopher Nolan, producers Emma Thomas and Charles Roven, actors Monique Gabriela Curnen, Michael Caine, Aaron Eckhart, Maggie Gyllenhaal and Christian Bale.

have to exorcise your demons." He added, "Now you have not just a young man in pain attempting to find some kind of an answer, you have somebody who actually has power, who is burdened by that power, and is having to recognize the difference between attaining that power and holding on to it." Bale felt Batman's personality had been strongly established in the first film, so it was unlikely his character would be overshadowed by the villains, stating: "I have no problem with competing with someone else. And that's going to make a better movie."

- Michael Caine as Alfred Pennyworth, Bruce's trusted butler and adviser. His supply of useful advice to Bruce and his likeness as a fatherly figure has led to him being labeled "Batman's batman."

- Heath Ledger as The Joker. Before Ledger was confirmed to play the Joker in July 2006, Paul Bettany, Lachy Hulme, Adrien Brody, Steve Carell, and Robin Williams publicly expressed interest in the role. Yet Nolan had wanted to work with Ledger on a number of projects in the past (though he had been unable to do so), and was agreeable to Ledger's chaotic interpretation of the character. When Ledger saw *Batman Begins*, he had realized a way to make the character work consistent with the film's tone: he described his Joker as a "psychopathic, mass murdering, schizophrenic clown with zero empathy."

To prepare for the role, Ledger lived alone in a hotel room for a month, formulating the character's posture, voice, and personality, and kept a diary, in which he recorded the Joker's thoughts and feelings. While he initially found it difficult, Ledger eventually generated a voice unlike Jack Nicholson's character in Tim Burton's 1989 *Batman* film. He was also given *Batman: The Killing Joke* and *Arkham Asylum: A Serious House on Serious Earth,* which he "really tried to read and put it down." Ledger also cited *A Clockwork Orange* and Sid Vicious as "a very early starting point for

Christian [Bale] and I. But we kind of flew far away from that pretty quickly and into another world altogether." "There's a bit of everything in him. There's nothing that consistent," Ledger said, and added, "There are a few more surprises to him." Ledger was allowed to shoot and mostly direct the videos the Joker sends out as warnings. Each take Ledger made was different from the last. Nolan was impressed enough with the first video shoot that he chose to not be present when Ledger shot the video with a kidnapped reporter (Anthony Michael Hall).

On January 22, 2008, after he had completed filming *The Dark Knight*, Ledger died of an accidental prescription drug overdose, leading to intense press attention and memorial tributes. "It was tremendously emotional, right when he passed, having to go back in and look at him every day [during editing]," Nolan recalled. "But the truth is, I feel very lucky to have something productive to do, to have a performance that he was very, very proud of, and that he had entrusted to me to finish." All of Ledger's scenes appear as he completed them in the filming; in editing the film, Nolan added no "digital effects" to alter Ledger's actual performance posthumously. Nolan has dedicated the film in part to Ledger's memory.

- Gary Oldman as James Gordon, a lieutenant in the Gotham City Police Department and one of the few police officers who is not corrupt. He forms a tenuous, unofficial alliance with Batman and Harvey. When the Joker assassinates Police Commissioner Loeb, Mayor Garcia gives Gordon the position. Oldman described his character as "incorruptible, virtuous, strong, heroic, but understated." Nolan explained that "*The Long Halloween* has a great, triangular relationship between Harvey Dent and Gordon and Batman, and that's something we very much drew from." Oldman added that "Gordon has a great deal of admiration for him at the end, but [Batman] is more than ever now the dark knight, the outsider. I'm intrigued now to see: If there is a third one, what he's going to do?" On the possibility of another sequel, he said that "returning to [the role] is not dependent on whether the role was bigger than the one before."

- Aaron Eckhart as Harvey Dent / Two-Face, the district attorney who is hailed as Gotham's "White Knight." Harvey's battle with the Joker transforms Harvey into a murderous, disfigured vigilante called "Two-Face." Wayne sees Dent as his heir, recognizing that Batman will be a lifelong mission, and heightening the tragedy of Dent's downfall. Nolan and David S. Goyer had originally considered using Dent in *Batman Begins*, but they replaced him with the new character Rachel Dawes when they realized they "couldn't do him justice." Before Eckhart was cast in February 2007, Liev Schreiber, Josh Lucas, and Ryan Phillippe had expressed interest in the role, while Mark Ruffalo auditioned. Hugh Jackman was also considered for the part of Harvey. Nolan chose Eckhart, whom he had considered for the lead role in *Memento*, citing his "extraordinary" ability as an actor, his embodiment of "that kind of chiselled, American hero quality" projected by Robert Redford, and his subtextual "edge."

Eckhart was "interested in good guys gone wrong," and had played corrupt men in films such as *The Black Dahlia*, *Thank You for Smoking*, and *In the Company of Men*. Whereas Two-Face is an evil villain in the comics, Nolan chose to portray him as a twisted vigilante to emphasize his role as Batman's counterpart. Eckhart explained, "[He] is still true to himself. He's a crime fighter, he's not killing good people. He's not a bad guy, not purely." For Dent, Eckhart "kept on thinking about the Kennedys," particularly Robert F. Kennedy, who was "idealistic, held a grudge and took on the Mob." He had his hair lightened and styled to make him appear more dashing. Nolan told Eckhart to not make Two-Face "jokey with slurping sounds or ticks."

- Maggie Gyllenhaal as Rachel Dawes, the Gotham assistant district attorney and Wayne's childhood friend. Before the events of the film, she told Wayne that if he ever decided to stop being Batman, they would be together. She is one of the few people to know Batman's identity. Gyllenhaal took over the role from Katie Holmes, who played it in *Batman Begins*. In August 2005, Holmes was reportedly planning to reprise the role, but she eventually turned it down to do *Mad Money* with Diane Keaton and Queen Latifah. By March 2007, Gyllenhaal was in "final talks" for the part. Gyllenhaal has acknowledged her character is a damsel in distress to an extent, but says Nolan sought ways to empower her character, so "Rachel's really clear about what's important to her and unwilling to compromise her morals, which made a nice change" from the many conflicted characters whom she has previously portrayed.

- Morgan Freeman as Lucius Fox, the recently-promoted chief executive officer of Wayne Enterprises who, now fully aware of his employer's double life, serves more directly as Bruce's armorer in addition to his corporate duties.

- Ng Chin Han as Lau, the accountant who handles the money for the mobs.

- Eric Roberts as Sal Maroni, a gangster who has taken over Carmine Falcone's mob. Bob Hoskins and James Gandolfini auditioned for the role.

- Colin McFarlane as Gillian B. Loeb, the Police Commissioner of Gotham until his murder at the hands of the Joker.

The film's Gotham officials and authorities include Nestor Carbonell as Mayor Anthony Garcia, Keith Szarabajka as Detective Gerard Stephens, Monique Gabriela Curnen as Anna Ramirez, and Ron Dean as Detective Michael Wuertz. While Stephens is an honest and good cop, the latter two are two corrupt officers who betray Harvey Dent and Rachel Dawes to the Joker. The film also cast Anthony Michael Hall as Gotham Cable News reporter Mike Engel, Nydia Rodriguez Terracina as Judge Janet Surrillo, Joshua Harto as Coleman Reese, Melinda McGraw and Nathan Gamble as Gordon's wife and son, and Tom "Tiny" Lister, Jr. as a prison inmate on one of the bomb-rigged ferries. The film's criminals include Michael Jai White as gang leader Gambol and Ritchie Coster as the Chechen. William Fichtner features as the Gotham National Bank manager. David Banner originally auditioned for the role of Gambol. Cillian Murphy returns in a cameo as Jonathan Crane / Scarecrow, who is captured early on in the film by Batman.

Musician Dwight Yoakam was approached for the roles of either the manager or a corrupt cop, but he chose to focus on his album *Dwight Sings Buck*. Another cameo was made by United States Senator

Patrick Leahy, a Batman fan who was previously an extra in the 1997 *Batman & Robin* and also was a guest voice actor on *Batman: The Animated Series*. Leahy cameos as a guest who defies the Joker at a fundraiser thrown by Bruce Wayne. Matt Skiba, lead singer of Chicago punk band Alkaline Trio made a small appearance in the movie.

Production

Development

As we looked through the comics, there was this fascinating idea that Batman's presence in Gotham actually attracts criminals to Gotham, [it] attracts lunacy. When you're dealing with questionable notions like people taking the law into their own hands, you have to really ask, where does that lead? That's what makes the character so dark, because he expresses a vengeful desire.

 Nolan on the theme of escalation

Before the release of *Batman Begins*, screenwriter David S. Goyer wrote a treatment for two sequels which introduced the Joker and Harvey Dent. His original intent was for the Joker to scar Dent during the Joker's trial in the third film, turning Dent into Two-Face. Goyer, who penned the first draft of the film, cited the DC Comics 13-issue comic book limited series *Batman: The Long Halloween* as the major influence on his storyline. While initially uncertain of whether or not he would return to direct the sequel, Nolan did want to reinterpret the Joker on screen. On July 31, 2006, Warner Bros. officially announced initiation of production for the sequel to *Batman Begins* titled *The Dark Knight*; it is the first live-action *Batman* film without the word "Batman" in its title, which Bale noted as signaling that "this take on Batman of mine and Chris' is very different from any of the others."

After much research, Nolan's brother and co-writer, Jonathan, suggested the Joker's first two appearances, published in the first issue of *Batman* (1940), as the crucial influences. Jerry Robinson, one of the Joker's co-creators, was consulted on the character's portrayal. Nolan decided to avoid divulging an in-depth origin story for the Joker, and instead portray his rise to power so as to not diminish the threat he poses, explaining to MTV News, "the Joker we meet in *The Dark Knight* is fully formed...To me, the Joker is an absolute. There are no shades of gray to him – maybe shades of purple. He's unbelievably dark. He bursts in just as he did in the comics." Nolan reiterated to IGN, "We never wanted to do an origin story for the Joker in this film," because "the arc of the story is much more Harvey Dent's; the Joker is presented as an absolute. It's a very thrilling element in the film, and a very important element, but we wanted to deal with the rise of the Joker, not the origin of the Joker." Nolan suggested *Batman: The Killing Joke* influenced a section of the Joker's dialogue in the film, in which he says that anyone can become like him given the right circumstances.

Nolan also cited *Heat* as "sort of an inspiration" for his aim "to tell a very large, city story or the story of a city": "If you want to take on Gotham, you want to give Gotham a kind of weight and breadth and depth in there. So you wind up dealing with the political figures, the media figures. That's part of the whole fabric of how a city is bound together."

According to Nolan, an important theme of the sequel is "escalation," extending the ending of *Batman Begins*, noting "things having to get worse before they get better." While indicating *The Dark Knight* would continue the themes of *Batman Begins*, including justice vs. revenge and Bruce Wayne's issues with his father, Nolan emphasized the sequel would also portray Wayne more as a detective, an aspect of his character not fully developed in *Batman Begins*. Nolan described the friendly rivalry between Bruce Wayne and Harvey Dent as the "backbone" of the film. He also chose to compress the overall storyline, allowing Dent to become Two-Face in *The Dark Knight*, thus giving the film an emotional arc the unsympathetic Joker could not offer. Nolan acknowledged the title was not only a reference to Batman, but also the fallen "white knight" Harvey Dent.

Filming

While scouting for shooting locations in October 2006, location manager Robin Higgs visited Liverpool, concentrating mainly along the city's waterfront. Other candidates included Yorkshire, Glasgow, and parts of London. In August 2006, one of the film's producers, Charles Roven, stated that its principal photography would begin in March 2007, but filming was pushed back to April. For its release in IMAX theaters, Nolan shot four major sequences in that format, including the Joker's introduction, and said that he wished that it were possible to shoot the entire film in IMAX: "if you could take an IMAX camera to Mount Everest or outer space, you could use it in a feature movie." For fifteen years Nolan had wanted to shoot in the IMAX format, and he also used it for "quiet scenes which pictorially we thought would be interesting."

Warner Bros. chose to film in Chicago for thirteen weeks, because Nolan had a "truly remarkable experience" filming part of *Batman Begins* there. Instead of using the Chicago Board of Trade Building as the location for the headquarters of Wayne Enterprises, as *Batman Begins* did, *The Dark Knight* used the Richard J. Daley Center. While filming in Chicago, the film was given the false title *Rory's First Kiss* to lower the visibility of production, but the local media eventually uncovered the ruse. Richard Roeper of the *Chicago Sun-Times* commented on the absurdity of the technique, "Is there a Bat-fan in the world that doesn't know *Rory's First Kiss* is actually *The Dark Knight*, which has been filming in Chicago for weeks?" Production of *The Dark Knight* in Chicago generated $45 million in the city's economy and created thousands of jobs. For the film's prologue involving the Joker, the crew shot in Chicago from April 18, 2007 to April 24, 2007. They returned to shoot from June 9, 2007 to early September. Shooting locations included Navy Pier, 330 North Wabash, James R. Thompson Center, LaSalle Street, The Berghoff, Millennium Station, Hotel 71, the old Brach's factory, the old Van Buren Street Post Office, and Wacker Drive. Pinewood Studios, near London, was the primary studio space used for the production. Marina City was in the background throughout the movie.

While planning a stunt with the Batmobile in a special effects facility near Chertsey, England in September 2007, technician Conway Wickliffe was killed when his car crashed. The film is dedicated to both Ledger and Wickliffe. The following month in London at the defunct Battersea Power Station, a rigged 200-foot fireball was filmed, reportedly for an opening sequence, prompting calls from local residents who feared a terrorist attack on the station. A similar incident occurred during the filming in Chicago, when an abandoned Brach's candy factory (which was Gotham Hospital in the film) was demolished.

Filming took place in Hong Kong from November 6 to November 11, 2007, at various locations in the CBD, including International Finance Centre, Hong Kong's tallest building. The city's walled city of Kowloon influenced the Narrows in *Batman Begins*. The shoot hired helicopters and C-130 aircraft. Officials expressed concern over possible noise pollution and traffic. In response, letters sent to the city's residents promised that the sound level would approximate noise decibels made by buses. Environmentalists also criticized the filmmakers' request to tenants of the waterfront skyscrapers to keep their lights on all night to enhance the cinematography, describing it as a waste of energy. Cinematographer Wally Pfister found the city officials a "nightmare," and ultimately Nolan had to create Batman's jump from a skyscraper digitally.

Design

Costume designer Lindy Hemming described the Joker's look as reflecting his personality − that "he doesn't care about himself at all"; she avoided designing him as a vagrant but still made him appear to be "scruffier, grungier," so that "when you see him move, he's slightly twitchier or edgy." Nolan noted, "We gave a Francis Bacon spin to [his face]. This corruption, this decay in the texture of the look itself. It's grubby. You can almost imagine what he smells like." In creating the "anarchical" look of the Joker, Hemming drew inspiration from such countercultural pop culture artists as Pete Doherty, Iggy Pop, and Johnny Rotten. Ledger described his "clown" mask, made up of three pieces of stamped silicone, as a "new technology," taking much less time for the make-up artists to apply than more-conventional prosthetics usually requires − the process took them only an hour − and said that he felt he was barely wearing any make-up. Hemming and Ledger's notable Joker design has had an impact in popular and political culture in the form of the Barack Obama "Joker" poster, and has since become a meme in its own right.

Designers improved on the design of the Batsuit from *Batman Begins*, adding wide elastic banding to help bind the costume to Bale, and suggest more sophisticated technology. It was constructed from 200 individual pieces of rubber, fiberglass, metallic mesh, and nylon. The new cowl was modeled after a motorcycle helmet and separated from the neck piece, allowing Bale to turn his head left and right and nod up and down. The cowl is equipped to show white lenses over the eyes when the character turns on his sonar detection, which gives Batman the white eyed look from the comics and animation. The gauntlets have retractable razors which can be fired. Though the new costume is eight pounds heavier, Bale found it more comfortable and less hot to wear. The original suit was also worn during part of the film, where Batman employs hydraulic assistance on the gauntlets to bend a gun barrel and cut through steel. Bruce Wayne drives a Lamborghini Murciélago in the film. 'Murciélago' means 'bat' in Spanish.

The depiction of Gotham City is less gritty than in *Batman Begins*. "I've tried to unclutter the Gotham we created on the last film," said Crowley. "Gotham is in chaos. We keep blowing up stuff, so we can keep our images clean."

Effects

A view of the "Batpod" on display in Los Angeles

The film introduces the Batpod, which is a recreation of the Batcycle. Production designer Nathan Crowley, who designed the Tumbler for *Batman Begins*, designed six models (built by special effects supervisor Chris Corbould) for use in the film's production, because of necessary crash scenes and possible accidents. Crowley built a prototype in Nolan's garage, before six months of safety tests were conducted. The Batpod is steered by shoulder instead of hand, and the rider's arms are protected by sleeve-like shields. The bike has 508-millimeter (20-inch) front and rear tires, and is made to appear as if it is armed with grappling hooks, cannons, and machine guns. The engines are located in the hubs of the wheels, which are set 3 1/2 feet (1067 mm) apart on either side of the tank. The rider lies belly down on the tank, which can move up and down to dodge any incoming gunfire that Batman may encounter. Stuntman Jean-Pierre Goy doubled for Christian Bale during the riding sequences in *The Dark Knight*.

Nolan designed Two-Face's appearance in the film as one of the least disturbing, explaining, "When we looked at less extreme versions of it, they were too real and more horrifying. When you look at a film like *Pirates of the Caribbean* – something like that, there's something about a very fanciful, very detailed visual effect, that I think is more powerful and less repulsive." Framestore created 120 computer-generated shots of Two-Face's scarred visage. Nolan felt using make-up would look unrealistic, as it adds to the face, unlike real burn victims. Framestore acknowledged they rearranged the positions of bones, muscles and joints to make the character look more dramatic. For each shot, three 720-pixel HD cameras were set up at different angles on set to fully capture Aaron Eckhart's performance. Eckhart wore markers on his face and a prosthetic skullcap, which acted as a lighting reference. A few shots of the skullcap were kept in the film. Framestore also integrated shots of Bale and Eckhart into that of the exploding building where Dent is burned. It was difficult simulating fire on Eckhart because only having half of something being burned is inherently unrealistic.

Music

See also: The Dark Knight (soundtrack)

Batman Begins composers Hans Zimmer and James Newton Howard returned to score the sequel. Composition began before shooting, and during filming Nolan received an iPod with ten hours of recordings. Their nine-minute suite for the Joker, "Why So Serious?," is based around two notes. Zimmer compared its style to that of Kraftwerk, a band from his native Germany, as well as bands like The Damned. When Ledger died, Zimmer felt like scrapping and composing a new theme, but decided that he could not be sentimental and compromise the "evil [performance] projects." Howard composed Dent's "elegant and beautiful" themes, which are brass-focused.

Marketing

In May 2007, 42 Entertainment began a viral marketing campaign utilizing the film's "Why So Serious?" tagline with the launch of a website featuring the fictional political campaign of Harvey Dent, with the caption, "I Believe in Harvey Dent." The site aimed to interest fans by having them try to earn what they wanted to see and, on behalf of Warner Bros., 42 Entertainment also established a "vandalized" version of *I Believe in Harvey Dent*, called "I believe in Harvey Dent too," where e-mails sent by fans slowly removed pixels, revealing the first official image of the Joker; it was ultimately replaced with many "Haha"s and a hidden message that said "see you in December."

During the 2007 San Diego Comic-Con International, 42 Entertainment launched WhySoSerious.com, sending fans on a scavenger hunt to unlock a teaser trailer and a new photo of the Joker. On October 31, 2007, the film's website morphed into another scavenger hunt with hidden messages, instructing fans to uncover clues at certain locations in major cities throughout the United States, and to take photographs of their discoveries. The clues combined to reveal a new photograph of the Joker and an audio clip of him from the film saying "And tonight, you're gonna break your one rule." Completing the scavenger hunt also led to another website called Rory's Death Kiss (referencing the false working title of *Rory's First Kiss*), where fans could submit photographs of themselves costumed as the Joker. Those who sent photos were mailed a copy of a fictional newspaper called *The Gotham Times*, whose electronic version led to the discovery of numerous other websites.

The Dark Knight's opening sequence, (showing a bank raid by the Joker) and closing montage of other scenes from the film, was screened with selected IMAX screenings of *I Am Legend*, which was released on December 14, 2007. A theatrical teaser was also released with non-IMAX showings of *I Am Legend*, and also on the official website. The sequence was released on the Blu-ray Disc edition of *Batman Begins* on July 8, 2008. Also on July 8, 2008, the studio released *Batman: Gotham Knight*, a direct-to-DVD animated film, set between *Batman Begins* and *The Dark Knight* and featuring six original stories, directed by Bruce Timm, co-creator and producer of *Batman: The Animated Series*, and starring veteran Batman voice actor Kevin Conroy. Each of these segments, written by Josh Olson, David S. Goyer, Brian Azzarello, Greg Rucka, Jordan Goldberg, and Alan Burnett, presents its own distinctive artistic style, paralleling numerous artists collaborating in the same DC Universe.

After the death of Heath Ledger on January 22, 2008, Warner Bros. adjusted its promotional focus on the Joker, revising some of its websites dedicated to promoting the film and posting a memorial tribute to Ledger on the film's official website and overlaying a black memorial ribbon on the photo collage in *WhySoSerious.com*. On February 29, 2008, *I Believe in Harvey Dent* was updated to enable fans to send their e-mail addresses and phone numbers. In March 2008, Harvey Dent's fictional campaign informed fans that actual campaign buses nicknamed "Dentmobiles" would tour various cities to promote Dent's candidacy for district attorney.

On May 15, 2008, Six Flags Great America and Six Flags Great Adventure theme parks opened *The Dark Knight* roller coaster, which cost US$7.5 million to develop and which simulates being stalked by the Joker. Mattel produced toys and games for *The Dark Knight*, action figures, role play costumes, board games, puzzles, and a special-edition UNO card game, which began commercial distribution in June 2008.

Toyota Formula One racing car featuring the Batman insignia, at the 2008 British Grand Prix

Warner Bros. devoted six months to an anti-piracy strategy that involved tracking the people who had a pre-release copy of the film at any one time. Shipping and delivery schedules were also staggered and spot checks were carried out both domestically and overseas to ensure illegal copying of the film was not taking place in cinemas. A pirated copy was released on the Web approximately 38 hours after the film's release. BitTorrent search engine The Pirate Bay taunted the movie industry over its ability to provide the movie free, replacing its logo with a taunting message.

Release

Warner Bros. held the world premiere for *The Dark Knight* in New York City on July 14, 2008, screening in an IMAX theater with the film's composers James Newton Howard and Hans Zimmer playing a part of the film score live. Leading up to *The Dark Knight*'s commercial release, the film had drawn "overwhelmingly positive early reviews and buzz on Heath Ledger's turn as the Joker." *The Dark Knight* was commercially released on July 16, 2008 in Australia, grossing almost $2.3 million in its first day.

In the United States and Canada, *The Dark Knight* was distributed to 4,366 theaters, breaking the previous record for the highest number of theaters held by *Pirates of the Caribbean: At World's End* in 2007. The number of theaters also included 94 IMAX theaters, with the film estimated to be played on 9,200 screens in the United States and Canada. Online, ticketing services sold enormous numbers of tickets for approximately 3,000 midnight showtimes as well as unusually early showtimes for the film's opening day. All IMAX theaters showing *The Dark Knight* were sold out for the opening weekend.

Reception

Based on 275 reviews collected by Rotten Tomatoes, the film received a 93% approval rating from critics, with an average score of 8.4/10. Among Rotten Tomatoes' *Top Critics*, which consists of popular and notable critics from the top newspapers, websites, television, and radio programs, the film holds an overall approval rating of 91%. By comparison, Metacritic, which assigns a normalized rating out of 100 top reviews from mainstream critics, calculated an average score of 82, based on 39 reviews. CinemaScore polls reported that the average grade cinemagoers gave the film was "A" on an A+ to F scale, and that audiences skewed slightly male and older.

Roger Ebert of the *Chicago Sun-Times* describes *The Dark Knight* as a "haunted film that leaps beyond its origins and becomes an engrossing tragedy." He praises the performances, direction, and writing, and says the film "redefine[s] the possibilities of the comic-book movie." Ebert states that the "key performance" is by Heath Ledger, and pondered whether he would become the first posthumous Academy Award-winning actor since Peter Finch in 1976. Ledger ultimately won the Oscar. He named it one of his twenty favorite films of 2008. Peter Travers of *Rolling Stone* writes that the film is deeper than its predecessor, with a "deft" script that refuses to scrutinize the Joker with popular psychology, instead pulling the viewer in with an examination of Bruce Wayne's psyche. Travers has praise for all the cast, saying each brings his or her "'A' game" to the film. He says Bale is "electrifying," evoking Al Pacino in *The Godfather Part II*, and that Eckhart's portrayal of Harvey Dent is "scarily moving." Travers says the actor moves the Joker away from Jack Nicholson's interpretation into darker territory, and expresses his support for any potential campaign to have Ledger nominated for an Academy Award, Travers says that the filmmakers move the film away from comic book cinema and closer to being a genuine work of art, citing Nolan's direction and the "gritty reality" of Wally Pfister's cinematography as helping to create a universe that has something "raw and elemental" at work within it. In particular, he cites Nolan's action choreography in the IMAX-tailored heist sequence as rivaling that of *Heat* (1995). *Entertainment Weekly* put it on its end-of-the-decade, "best-of" list, saying, "Every great hero needs a great villain. And in 2008, Christian Bale's Batman found his in Heath Ledger's demented dervish, the Joker."

Emanuel Levy wrote Ledger "throws himself completely" into the role, and that the film represents Nolan's "most accomplished and mature" work, and the most technically impressive and resonant of all the *Batman* films. Levy calls the action sequences some of the most impressive seen in an American film for years, and talks of the Hong Kong-set portion of the film as being particularly visually impressive. Levy and Peter Travers conclude that the film is "haunting and visionary," while Levy goes on to say that *The Dark Knight* is "nothing short of brilliant." On the other hand, David Denby of *The New Yorker* holds that the story is not coherent enough to properly flesh out the disparities. He says the film's mood is one of "constant climax," and that it feels rushed and far too long. Denby criticizes scenes which he argues are meaningless or are cut short just as they become interesting. Denby remarks that the central conflict is workable, but that "only half the team can act it," saying that Bale's "placid"

Bruce Wayne and "dogged but uninteresting" Batman is constantly upstaged by Ledger's "sinister and frightening" performance, which he says is the film's one element of success. Denby concludes that Ledger is "mesmerising" in every scene. While Denby has praise for Pfister's cinematography, he does not rate the film as a remarkable piece of craftmanship. He puts forward that while a lot happens in the film, it is often difficult to follow due to the close, dark photography and editing. Denby says the film is too grim and is seemingly "jammed together." He surmises that the "heavy-handed" score and "thunderous" violence only serve to coarsen the property from Tim Burton's vision of the franchise into a "hyperviolent summer action spectacle," and that the film embraces the themes of terror that it purports to scrutinize.

The Dark Knight was ranked the 15th greatest film in history on *Empire's* 2008 list of the "500 Greatest Movies of All Time," based upon the weighted votes of 10,000 readers, 150 film directors, and 50 key film critics. Heath Ledger's interpretation of the Joker was also ranked number three on *Empire*'s 2008 list of the "100 Greatest Movie Characters of All Time."

Top ten lists

The film appeared on many critics' top ten lists of the best films of 2008.

- 1st – Elizabeth Weitzman, *New York Daily News*
- 1st – Frank Scheck, *The Hollywood Reporter*
- 1st – James Berardinelli, ReelViews
- 1st – Joe Neumaier, *New York Daily News*
- 1st – Mike Russell, *The Oregonian*
- 1st – Peter Hartlaub, *San Francisco Chronicle*
- 1st – *Premiere*
- 1st – *Empire*
- 2nd – Kirk Honeycutt, *The Hollywood Reporter*
- 2nd – Nathan Rabin, *The A.V. Club*
- 2nd – Richard Roeper, *Chicago Sun-Times*
- 2nd – Owen Gleiberman, *Entertainment Weekly*
- 3rd – Lawrence Toppman, *The Charlotte Observer*
- 3rd – Lisa Schwarzbaum, *Entertainment Weekly*
- 3rd – Marc Mohan, *The Oregonian*
- 3rd – Michael Rechtshaffen, *The Hollywood Reporter*
- 3rd – Peter Rainer, *The Christian Science Monitor*
- 3rd – Peter Travers, *Rolling Stone*
- 3rd – Sheri Linden, *The Hollywood Reporter*
- 4th – Kyle Smith, *New York Post*
- 5th – Keith Phipps, *The A.V. Club*
- 5th – Noel Murray, *The A.V. Club*
- 5th – Rene Rodriguez, *The Miami Herald* (tied with *Hellboy II*)
- 5th – Scott Foundas, *LA Weekly*
- 5th – Wesley Morris, *The Boston Globe*
- 6th – Philip Martin, *Arkansas Democrat-Gazette*
- 6th – Peter Vonder Haar, *Film Threat*
- 7th – Manohla Dargis, *The New York Times*
- 7th – Marc Doyle, Metacritic
- 7th – Sean Axmaker, *Seattle Post-Intelligencer*
- 9th – Robert Mondello, *NPR*
- 9th – Scott Tobias, *The A.V. Club*
- 10th – Michael Phillips, *Chicago Tribune*

Commentary

Mystery writer Andrew Klavan, writing in *The Wall Street Journal*, compared the extreme measures that Batman takes to fight crime with those U.S. President George W. Bush used in the War on Terror. Klavan claims that, "at some level" *The Dark Knight* is "a paean of praise to the fortitude and moral courage that has been shown by George W. Bush in this time of terror and war." Klavan supports this reading of the film by comparing Batman – like Bush, Klavan argues – "sometimes has to push the boundaries of civil rights to deal with an emergency, certain that he will re-establish those boundaries when the emergency is past." Klavan's article has received criticism on the Internet and in mainstream media outlets, such as in *The New Republic's* "The Plank." Reviewing the film in *The Sunday Times*, Cosmo Landesman reached the opposite conclusion to Klavan, arguing that *The Dark Knight* "offers up a lot of moralistic waffle about how we must hug a terrorist – okay, I exaggerate. At its heart, however, is a long and tedious discussion about how individuals and society must never abandon the rule of law in struggling against the forces of lawlessness. In fighting monsters, we must be careful not to become monsters – that sort of thing. The film champions the anti-war coalition's claim that, in having a war on terror, you create the conditions for more terror. We are shown that innocent people died because of Batman – and he falls for it." Benjamin Kerstein, writing in *Azure*, says that both Klavan and Landesman "have a point," because "*The Dark Knight* is a perfect mirror of the society which is watching it: a society so divided on the issues of terror and how to fight it that, for the first time in decades, an American mainstream no longer exists."

Themes and analysis

According to David S. Goyer, the primary theme of *The Dark Knight* is escalation. Gotham City is weak and the citizens blame Batman for the city's violence and corruption as well as the Joker's threats, and it pushes his limits, making him feel that taking the laws into his own hands is further downgrading the city. Roger Ebert noted, "Throughout the film, [the Joker] devises ingenious situations that force Batman, Commissioner Gordon and District Attorney Harvey Dent to make impossible ethical decisions. By the end, the whole moral foundation of the Batman legend is threatened."

Other critics have mentioned the theme of the triumph of evil over good. Harvey Dent is seen as Gotham's "White Knight" in the beginning of the film but ends up becoming seduced to evil. The Joker, on the other hand, is seen as the representation of anarchy and chaos. He has no motive, no orders, and no desires but to cause havoc and "watch the world burn." The terrible logic of human error is another theme as well. The ferry scene displays how humans can easily be enticed by iniquity.

Accolades

Main article: List of accolades received by The Dark Knight

The *Tumbler* in use at the film's European premiere

Most notable among the nominations were Heath Ledger's almost complete sweep of over twenty awards for acting, including the Academy Award for Best Supporting Actor, Screen Actors Guild Award for Best Supporting Actor, the Golden Globe Award for Best Supporting Actor – Motion Picture, and the BAFTA Award for Best Actor in a Supporting Role. *The Dark Knight* also received nominations from the Writers Guild of America (for Best Adapted Screenplay), the Producers Guild of America, and the Directors Guild of America, as well as a slew of other guild award nominations and wins. It was nominated for Best Film at the Critics Choice Awards and was named one of the top ten films of 2008 by the American Film Institute.

The Dark Knight was nominated for eight Academy Awards for the 81st Ceremony, breaking the previous record of seven held by *Dick Tracy* for the most nominations received by a film based on a comic book, comic strip, or graphic novel. *The Dark Knight* won two awards: Best Supporting Actor for Heath Ledger and Best Sound Editing. It was additionally nominated for six others, these being Best Art Direction, Best Cinematography, Best Sound Mixing, Best Visual Effects, Best Makeup, and Best Film Editing. Heath Ledger was the first posthumous winner of the Best Supporting Actor award, and only the second posthumous acting winner ever (Peter Finch posthumously won the Best Actor award for his performance in the 1976 film *Network*). In addition, Ledger's win marked the first win in any of the major Oscar categories (producing, directing, acting, or writing) for a superhero-based film. Notably, Richard King's win in the Sound Editing category blocked a complete awards sweep of the evening by the eventual Best Picture winner, *Slumdog Millionaire*. Although it did not receive a Best Picture nomination, the show's opening song paid homage to *The Dark Knight* along with the five Best Picture nominees, including host Hugh Jackman riding on a mockup of the Batpod made out of garbage.

Box office

The Dark Knight set a new midnight record on the opening day of July 18, 2008 with $18.5 million, beating the $16.9 million record set by *Star Wars Episode III: Revenge of the Sith* in 2005. $640,000 of the record gross came from IMAX screenings. However, this record was broken a year later by the film *Harry Potter and the Half-Blood Prince*, which grossed over $22 million.

The Dark Knight ultimately grossed $67,165,092 on its opening day in the domestic office, beating the previous record of $59.8 million held by *Spider-Man 3* in 2007. However, the record was broken by *The Twilight Saga: New Moon* a year later, which grossed close to $73 million.

For its opening weekend in the United States and Canada, *The Dark Knight* accumulated a total of $158,411,483 from 9,200 screens at a record 4,366 theaters, for an average of $36,283 per theater, or $17,219 per screen, beating out the original weekend estimate by more than $3 million, and topping the previous record of $151,116,516 held by *Spider-Man 3*, while playing in 114 more theaters but on 800 fewer screens. The following Monday, it grossed another $24,493,313, and the following Tuesday it grossed $20,868,722. *The Dark Knight* also set a new record for opening weekend gross in IMAX theaters, accumulating $6.2 million to beat *Spider-Man 3*'s previous record of $4.7 million.

Besides the United States and Canada, *The Dark Knight* premiered in 20 other territories on 4,520 screens, grossing $41.3 million in its first weekend. The film came in second to *Hancock*, which was in its third weekend, screening in 71 territories. *The Dark Knight*'s biggest territory for the weekend was Australia, grossing $13.7 million over the weekend, the third largest Warner Bros. opening and the largest superhero film opening to date. The film also grossed $7 million from 1,433 screens in Mexico, $4.45 million from 548 screens in Brazil, and $2.12 million from 37 screens in Hong Kong. Citing cultural sensitivities to some elements in the film, and a reluctance to adhere to pre-release conditions, Warner Bros. declined to release the film in mainland China.

A sign of the film's pre-release at the cinema *Colisevm* in Barcelona, Spain

The Dark Knight sold an estimated 22.37 million tickets with today's average admission of $7.08, meaning the film sold more tickets than *Spider-Man 3*, which sold 21.96 million with the average price of $6.88 in 2007. It also broke the record for the biggest opening week ever. As of December 23, 2008, *The Dark Knight* had grossed $530,833,780 in the North American box office, in the process becoming the second film to gross more than $500 million in the North American box office, after *Titanic*, and doing so in significantly less time. It had also grossed $465,993,073 in other countries. As of August 29, 2010, its total worldwide gross stands at $1,001,758,644, and is the seventh highest-grossing film of all time (unadjusted for inflation). *The Dark Knight* is the highest-grossing film of 2008 in North American box office and worldwide. Unadjusted for inflation, it is the third highest-grossing film of all time in North America with a total of $533,090,262, behind only *Avatar* and *Titanic*. *The Dark Knight*'s theatrical run was very different from that of *Avatar*, which broke some of its records, and *Titanic*, at the time the only movie to gross more in North America than it. While *The Dark Knight* broke records in its opening weekend, *Titanic* started out slowly (making $28.6 million in its opening weekend) and then increased ticket sales in the following weekends. *The Dark Knight* instead slowed down after the first few weekends; 50 other movies had better tenth weekends and 91 had better eleventh weekends. In its fifteenth weekend, *The Dark Knight* was at #26 at the box office.

Warner Bros. re-released the film in traditional theaters and IMAX theaters in the United States on January 23, 2009, at the height of the voting for the Academy Awards, to further the chances of the film winning Oscars, as well as attempt to cross $1 billion in worldwide gross, which it accomplished in February 2009.

Home media

The film was released on DVD and Blu-ray Disc in North America on December 9, 2008. Releases include a one-disc edition DVD; a two-disc Special Edition DVD; a two-disc edition BD; and a Special Edition BD package featuring a statuette of the Bat-pod. The BD version presents the film in a variable aspect ratio, with the IMAX sequences framed in 1.78:1, while scenes filmed in 35 mm are framed in 2.40:1. The DVD versions feature the entire film framed in a uniform 2.40:1 aspect ratio. Disc 2 of the two-disc Special Edition DVD features the six main IMAX sequences in the original 1.44:1 aspect ratio. Additional IMAX shots throughout the film that are presented in 1.78:1 on the Blu-Ray release are not, however, included in the DVD's special features. In addition to the standard DVD releases, some stores released their own exclusive editions of the film.

In the United Kingdom, the film had combined sales of 513,000 units on its first day of release, of which 107,730 (21%) were Blu-ray Discs, the highest number of first-day Blu-ray Discs sold. In the United States, *The Dark Knight* set a sales record for most DVDs sold in one day, selling 3 million units on its first day of release – 600,000 of which were Blu-ray Discs.

The DVD and Blu-ray Disc editions were released in Australia on December 10, 2008. Releases were in the form of a one-disc edition on DVD; a two-disc edition on DVD; a two-disc edition including a Batmask on DVD and BD; a two-disc Batpod statuette Limited BD Edition; a two-disc BD edition; and a four-disc *Batman Begins/The Dark Knight* pack on DVD and BD. As of December 19, 2008, the DVD release is the top selling film in the Australian DVD Charts and is expected to break the Australian sales record set by *Finding Nemo*.

Sequel

On March 10, 2010, Nolan confirmed his involvement with a sequel and gave some information regarding the story. The next Batman film will be Nolan's last and a conclusion to the story. Nolan says, "Without getting into specifics, the key thing that makes the third film a great possibility for us is that we want to finish our story. And in viewing it as the finishing of a story rather than infinitely blowing up the balloon and expanding the story . . . I'm very excited about the end of the film, the conclusion, and what we've done with the characters. My brother has come up with some pretty exciting stuff. Unlike the comics, these things don't go on forever in film and viewing it as a story with an end is useful. Viewing it as an ending, that sets you very much on the right track about the appropriate conclusion and the essence of what tale we're telling. And it hearkens back to that priority of trying to find the reality in these fantastic stories. That's what we do." Nolan has also confirmed that

Jonathan Nolan is writing the script and that the villain of the film "won't be Mr. Freeze." Nolan also confirmed that the Joker will not return.

In April 2010, Warner Bros. announced the as-yet-untitled sequel will be released on July 20, 2012. Nolan confirmed in an interview in July 2010 that his brother Jonathan has finished a screenplay that was based on a story by Nolan and David Goyer. Nolan is also still aiming for a 2012 release date. The film will begin shooting in April 2011. Christopher Nolan's long-time cinematographer Wally Pfister has expressed interest in shooting the entirety of the next Batman movie in the IMAX format, as both Pfister and Nolan have expressed distaste for shooting the film in 3-D. Nolan has confirmed that he will be directing the film and stated that he is currently polishing Jonathan Nolan's screenplay.

Further reading

- Byrne, Craig (2008) (Hardcover). *The Dark Knight: Featuring Production Art and Full Shooting Script*. Universe. ISBN 0789318121.
- Nolan, Christopher; David S. Goyer (2007). "Introduction" (Hardcover). *Absolute Batman: The Long Halloween*. New York: DC Comics. ISBN 1401212824.
- O'Neil, Dennis (2008) (Paperback). *The Dark Knight*. Novelization of the film. Berkley. ISBN 0425222861.

External links

- Official website [1]
- *The Dark Knight* [2] at the Internet Movie Database
- *The Dark Knight* [3] at Allmovie
- *The Dark Knight* [8] at Box Office Mojo
- *The Dark Knight* [4] at MySpace
- *The Dark Knight* [5] at Rotten Tomatoes
- *The Dark Knight* [6] at Metacritic
- *The Dark Knight: Blu-ray Disc Review"* [7] at HD Report
- Official site script [8]

Inception (film)

Inception	
Theatrical release poster	
Directed by	Christopher Nolan
Produced by	Christopher Nolan Emma Thomas
Written by	Christopher Nolan
Starring	Leonardo DiCaprio Ken Watanabe Joseph Gordon-Levitt Marion Cotillard Ellen Page Tom Hardy Cillian Murphy Tom Berenger Michael Caine
Music by	Hans Zimmer
Cinematography	Wally Pfister
Editing by	Lee Smith
Studio	Legendary Pictures Syncopy Films
Distributed by	Warner Bros. Pictures
Release date(s)	July 8, 2010 (London premiere) July 16, 2010 (United States)
Running time	148 minutes
Country	United States
Language	English
Budget	$160 million
Gross revenue	$804,183,607

Inception is a 2010 American science fiction film written, produced, and directed by Christopher Nolan. The film stars Leonardo DiCaprio, Ken Watanabe, Joseph Gordon-Levitt, Marion Cotillard, Ellen Page, Tom Hardy, Cillian Murphy, Tom Berenger, and Michael Caine. DiCaprio plays Dom

Cobb, a thief who extracts information from the unconscious mind of his victims while they dream. Unable to visit his children, Cobb is offered a chance to regain his old life in exchange for one last job: performing inception, the planting of an idea into the mind of his client's competitor.

Development began roughly nine years before *Inception* was released. In 2001, Nolan wrote an 80-page treatment about dream-stealers, presenting the idea to Warner Bros. The story was originally written as a heist film, inspired by concepts of lucid dreaming and dream incubation. Feeling he needed to have more experience with large-scale films, Nolan opted to work on *Batman Begins*, *The Prestige* and *The Dark Knight*. He spent six months polishing up the script for *Inception* before Warner Bros. purchased it in February 2009. Filming spanned six countries and four continents, beginning in Tokyo on June 19, 2009 and finishing in Canada in late November of the same year. Composer Hans Zimmer scored the film, using parts of Edith Piaf's song "Non, je ne regrette rien".

Inception was officially budgeted at $160 million, a cost that was split between Warner Bros. and Legendary Pictures. Nolan's reputation and success with *The Dark Knight* helped secure the film's $100 million in advertising expenditure. *Inception* premiered in London on July 8, 2010 and was released in both conventional and IMAX theaters on July 14, 2010. Released to critical acclaim, the film grossed over $21 million on its opening day, with an opening weekend gross of $62.7 million.

Plot

Dom Cobb (Leonardo DiCaprio), along with point man Arthur (Joseph Gordon-Levitt), are on an extraction mission within the mind of a powerful Japanese businessman Saito (Ken Watanabe); a form of corporate espionage through dreams. Pain is felt in dreams, but death results in awakening. Cobb carries a totem in the form of a spinning top which originally belonged to his deceased wife Mal (Marion Cotillard), to determine whether he is dreaming or awake, which spins unceasingly or topples, respectively. The extraction fails due to the intervention of Mal, whose memory haunts Cobb's mind and sabotages his missions. Saito reveals that he is in fact auditioning the team to perform the act of inception: using dreams to implant an idea. He promises to have murder charges against Cobb cleared so that he can return to the U.S. and visit his children, in return for the mission's success.

The target is Robert Fischer (Cillian Murphy), son of Saito's terminally ill corporate rival, Maurice Fischer (Pete Postlethwaite). The objective is to convince Fischer to break up his father's empire. Cobb recruits Eames (Tom Hardy), a forger who can change appearance inside dreams, Yusuf (Dileep Rao), a sedative chemist, and Ariadne (Ellen Page), a student whom he and Arthur train as an architect to design dream worlds. When the elder Fischer dies in Sydney, Saito and the team share the flight with Robert Fischer back to Los Angeles and drug him. They enter Yusuf's dream, a rainy downtown area, and kidnap Fischer. However, they come under attack by Fischer's trained unconscious mind projections, and Saito is badly injured. Due to the strength of the sedatives and multiple dream layers, death will result in the person going into limbo, a world of unconstructed dream space, for a seemingly indefinite time. Cobb reveals to Ariadne that he spent years with Mal in limbo, where they shaped their own world and lives. After waking, Mal remained convinced she was dreaming and committed suicide, persuading Cobb to do so by incriminating him in her death, but he instead fled the U.S. and the murder charges.

Eames changes into Peter Browning (Tom Berenger), Fischer's godfather, to extract information from him. The team then enter a van and are sedated into Arthur's dream, a hotel, where the team convinces Fischer that the kidnapping on the first level was orchestrated by Browning and that he must enter his godfather's mind to determine his motives. They in fact enter into a third level of Fischer's dream, where Fischer must break into a snowy mountain fortress to reveal the planted idea. To wake and protect the team, a member stays behind at each level with synchronized kicks: Yusuf driving the van off a bridge, Arthur crashing an elevator containing the team's bodies in a zero gravity sequence, and Eames detonating explosives in the mountain fortress.

Fischer is killed by Mal and goes into limbo. Ariadne and Cobb follow him down and confront her. There Mal attempts to convince Cobb to stay in limbo by making him question reality, referring to events that occurred while he was awake. Cobb reveals that he had originally planted the idea in Mal's mind to wake, making him indirectly responsible for her suicide. She attacks him, but Ariadne shoots her. Cobb remains in limbo to locate a now dead Saito, while Fischer and Ariadne return to the mountain fortress where he comes to the conclusion that his father wanted him to be his own man. Cobb eventually locates an aged Saito and tells him that they need to return to reality. He suddenly wakes on the plane to find everyone up and well. Saito honors their arrangement; Cobb enters the United States and finally returns home to his children. Cobb spins his totem top to test reality, but is distracted by the reunion.

Cast

- Leonardo DiCaprio as Dominic Cobb, the Extractor, a professional thief who specializes in conning secrets from his victims by infiltrating their dreams. Cobb leads a team consisting of Arthur, Ariadne, Eames, Saito, and Yusuf, with the goal of influencing Fischer's actions via his dreams.

The cast at a premiere for the film in July 2010. From left to right: Cillian Murphy, Marion Cotillard, Joseph Gordon-Levitt, Ellen Page, Ken Watanabe, Michael Caine, and Leonardo DiCaprio.

- Ellen Page as Ariadne, the Architect, a graduate student who is recruited to construct the various dream-scapes, which are described as mazes. The name Ariadne alludes to a princess of Greek myth, daughter of King Minos, who aided the hero Theseus by giving him a sword and a ball of string to help him navigate the labyrinth which was the prison of the Minotaur.

- Marion Cotillard as Mallorie Cobb, the Shade, Dom Cobb's projection of his deceased wife and a frequent, malevolent presence in his dreams. The film's main antagonist, she is a manifestation of his guilt about the real Mal's suicide. Dom is unable to control these projections of her, challenging his abilities as an extractor.

- Joseph Gordon-Levitt as Arthur, the Point Man, Cobb's partner and the man responsible for researching the team's targets.
- Ken Watanabe as Mr. Saito, the Tourist, a businessman who employs Cobb for the team's mission, and insists on joining them inside.
- Tom Hardy as Eames, the Forger, a sharp-tongued associate of Cobb's. Eames uses his ability to take the form of others in order to manipulate Fischer in Fischer's dreams.
- Dileep Rao as Yusuf, the Chemist, who formulates the drugs needed to sustain the dream states.
- Cillian Murphy as Robert Michael Fischer Jr., the Mark, the heir to a business empire and the team's target.
- Tom Berenger as Peter Browning, Fischer's godfather and fellow executive at the Fischers' company.
- Michael Caine as Prof. Stephen Miles, Cobb's mentor and father-in-law, and Ariadne's college professor who recommends her to the team.
- Pete Postlethwaite as Maurice Fischer, Robert's dying father.
- Lukas Haas as Nash, an architect in Cobb's employment who is replaced by Ariadne.
- Miranda Nolan plays a minor role as an air hostess. Miranda is a first cousin to the film's director Christopher Nolan.

Production

Origins

Inception was first developed by Christopher Nolan, based on the notion of "exploring the idea of people sharing a dream space — entering a dream space and sharing a dream. That gives you the ability to access somebody's unconscious mind. What would that be used and abused for?" Furthermore, he thought "being able to extract information from somebody's brain would be the obvious use of that because obviously any other system where it's computers or physical media, whatever — things that exist outside the mind — they can all be stolen ... up until this point, or up until this movie I should say, the idea that you could actually steal something from somebody's head was impossible. So that, to me, seemed a fascinating abuse or misuse of that kind of technology." Nolan drew inspiration from the works of Jorge Luis Borges when writing *Inception*.

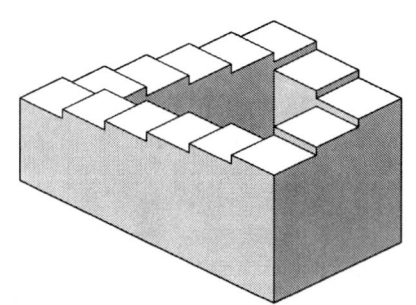

Penrose stairs are incorporated into the film as an example of the impossible objects that can be created in lucid dream worlds.

Nolan had thought about these ideas on and off since he was sixteen years old, intrigued by how he would wake up and then, while falling back into a lighter sleep, hold on to the awareness that he was dreaming, a lucid dream. He also became aware of the feeling that he could study the place and alter the events of the dream. He said, "I tried to work that idea of manipulation and management of a conscious dream being a skill that these people have. Really the script is based on those common, very basic experiences and concepts, and where can those take you? And the only outlandish idea that the film presents, really, is the existence of a technology that allows you to enter and share the same dream as someone else." Harvard University dream researcher Deirdre Barrett points out that Nolan did not get every detail accurate regarding dreams, but that films which really do that tend to have illogical, rambling, disjointed plots which wouldn't make for a great thriller. "But he did get many aspects right," she said, citing the scene in which a sleeping DiCaprio is shoved into a full bath and water starts gushing into the windows of the building he is dreaming, waking him up. "That's very much how real stimuli get incorporated, and you very often wake up right after that intrusion."

Development

Initially, Nolan wrote an 80-page treatment about dream-stealers. Originally, Nolan had envisioned *Inception* as a horror film, but eventually wrote it as a heist film even though he found that "traditionally [they] are very deliberately superficial in emotional terms." Upon revisiting his script, he decided that basing it in that genre did not work because the story "relies so heavily on the idea of the interior state, the idea of dream and memory. I realized I needed to raise the emotional stakes." Nolan worked on the script for nine to ten years. When he first started thinking about making the film, Nolan was influenced by "that era of movies where you had *The Matrix*, you had *Dark City*, you had *The Thirteenth Floor* and, to a certain extent, you had *Memento*, too. They were based in the principles that the world around you might not be real."

Nolan first pitched the film to Warner Bros. in 2001, but then felt that he needed more experience making large-scale films, and embarked on *Batman Begins* and *The Dark Knight*. He soon realized that a film like *Inception* needed a large budget because "as soon as you're talking about dreams, the potential of the human mind is infinite. And so the scale of the film has to feel infinite. It has to feel like you could go anywhere by the end of the film. And it has to work on a massive scale." After making *The Dark Knight*, Nolan decided to make *Inception* and spent six months completing the script. Nolan states that the key to completing the script was wondering what would happen if several people shared the same dream. "Once you remove the privacy, you've created an infinite number of alternative universes in which people can meaningfully interact, with validity, with weight, with dramatic consequences."

Leonardo DiCaprio was the first actor to be cast in the film. Nolan had been trying to work with the actor for years and met him several times, but was unable to convince him to appear in any of his films until *Inception*. DiCaprio finally agreed because he was "intrigued by this concept — this dream-heist notion and how this character's going to unlock his dreamworld and ultimately affect his real life." He read the script and found it to be "very well written, comprehensive but you really had to have Chris in person, to try to articulate some of the things that have been swirling around his head for the last eight years." DiCaprio and Nolan spent months talking about the screenplay. Nolan took a long time re-writing the script in order "to make sure that the emotional journey of his character was the driving force of the movie." On February 11, 2009, it was announced that Warner Bros. purchased *Inception*, a spec script written by Nolan.

Filming

Principal photography began in Tokyo on June 19, 2009 for the scene where Saito first hires Cobb during a helicopter flight over the city. The production moved to England and shot in Cardington, a converted airship hangar north of London. It was there that a hotel bar set was constructed that could be tilted 30 degrees. A long hotel corridor was also constructed by production designer Guy Hendrix Dyas, special effects supervisor Chris Corbould, and cinematographer Wally Pfister; this corridor was able to rotate a full 360 degrees to create the effect of alternate directions of gravity for scenes where dream-sector physics become chaotic. This idea was inspired by a similar technique used in Stanley Kubrick's *2001: A Space Odyssey*. Nolan said, "I was interested in taking those ideas, techniques and philosophies and applying them to an action scenario". The filmmakers originally planned to make the hallway 40 ft (12 m) long but as the action sequence became more elaborate, the hallway's length grew to 100 ft (30 m). The corridor was suspended along eight large concentric rings that were spaced equidistantly outside its walls and powered by two massive electric motors. Joseph Gordon-Levitt, who plays Arthur, spent several weeks learning to fight in a corridor that spun like "a giant hamster wheel". Nolan said of the device, "It was like some incredible torture device; we thrashed Joseph for weeks, but in the end we looked at the footage, and it looks unlike anything any of us has seen before. The rhythm of it is unique, and when you watch it, even if you know how it was done, it confuses your perceptions. It's unsettling in a wonderful way". Gordon-Levitt remembered, "it was six-day weeks of just, like, coming home at night fuckin' battered ... The light fixtures on the ceiling are coming around on the floor, and you have to choose the right time to cross through them, and if you don't, you're going to fall." On July 15, 2009, filming took place at University College London library. The signage of the library was changed to read "bibliothèque" (French for "library").

Filming moved to France where they shot the pivotal scene between Ariadne and Cobb at a Paris bistro. For the explosion that takes place during this scene, the local authorities would not allow the actual use of explosives. The production used high-pressure nitrogen to create the effect of a series of explosions. Pfister used six high-speed cameras to capture the sequence from different angles and make sure that they got the shot. The visual effects department enhanced the sequence, adding more destruction and flying debris. The next location that the production traveled to was Tangiers which doubled for Mombasa, where Cobb hires Eames and Yusuf. A foot chase was shot in the streets and alleyways of the historic Grand Souk. To capture this sequence, Pfister employed a mix of hand-held camera and

Steadicam work. Tangiers was also used to film an important riot scene during the initial foray into Saito's mind.

Filming moved to the Los Angeles area where some sets were built on a Warner Bros. sound stage, including the interior rooms of Saito's Japanese-style castle. The dining room was inspired by the Nijo Castle built around 1603. These sets were inspired by a mix of Japanese architecture and Western influences. The production also staged a multi-vehicle car chase on the streets of downtown L.A. and this also involved bringing a freight train down the middle of a street. To do this, the filmmakers configured a train engine on the chassis of a tractor trailer. The replica was made from fiberglass molds taken from authentic train parts and then matched in terms of color and design. Also, the car chase was supposed to be set in the midst of a downpour but the L.A. weather stayed typically sunny. The filmmakers were forced to set up elaborate effects (e.g., rooftop water cannons) to give the audience the impression that the weather was overcast and soggy. L.A. was also the site of the climactic scene where a Ford Econoline van flies off the Commodore Schuyler F. Heim Bridge in slow motion. This sequence was filmed on and off for months with the van being shot out of a cannon according to actor Dileep Rao. Capturing the actors suspended within the van in slow motion took a whole day to film. Once the van landed in the water the challenge for the actors was not to panic. According to Cillian Murphy, "And when they ask you to act, it's a bit of an ask." The actors had to hold their breath for four to five minutes while drawing air from scuba tanks.

The final phase of principal photography took place near Calgary, Alberta, Canada in late November 2009. The location manager discovered a temporarily closed ski resort known as the Fortress Mountain Resort. An elaborate set was assembled near the top station of the Canadian chairlift, taking three months to build. The production had to wait for a huge snowstorm, which eventually arrived. The ski-chase sequence was inspired by Nolan's favorite James Bond film, *On Her Majesty's Secret Service*: "What I liked about it that we've tried to emulate in this film is there's a tremendous balance in that movie of action and scale and romanticism and tragedy and emotion."

The film was shot primarily in the anamorphic format on 35 mm film, with key sequences filmed on 65 mm, and certain other sequences in VistaVision. Nolan did not shoot any footage with IMAX cameras as he had with *The Dark Knight*. "We didn't feel that we were going to be able to shoot in IMAX because of the size of the cameras because this film given that it deals with a potentially surreal area, the nature of dreams and so forth, I wanted it to be as realistic as possible. Not be bound by the scale of those IMAX cameras, even though I love the format dearly". Nolan also chose not to shoot any of the film in 3-D as he believes that shooting on digital video does not offer a high enough quality image. Cinematographer Wally Pfister gave each location and dream level a distinctive look with the mountain fortress having a sterile, cool look, the hotel hallways had warm hues and the van scenes were neutral. This was done so that the audience would know immediately where they were during the heavily crosscut portion of the film.

Nolan has said that the film "deals with levels of reality, and perceptions of reality which is something I'm very interested in. It's an action film set in a contemporary world, but with a slight science-fiction bent to it," while also describing it as "very much an ensemble film structured somewhat as a heist movie. It's an action adventure that spans the globe".

Visual effects

For dream sequences in *Inception*, Nolan kept the computer-generated effects to a minimum and preferred to use practical methods whenever possible. Nolan said, "It's always very important to me to do as much as possible in-camera, and then, if necessary, computer graphics are very useful to build on or enhance what you have achieved physically." To this end, visual effects supervisor Paul Franklin built a miniature of the Fortress Mountain Resort set and then blew it up for the film. For the fight scene that takes place in zero g, he used CG-based effects to "subtly bend elements like physics, space and time."

The most challenging effect was Limbo City at the end of the film because it continually developed during production. Franklin had artists build concepts while Nolan gave his ideal vision: "Something glacial, with clear modernist architecture, but with chunks of it breaking off into the sea like icebergs". Franklin and his team ended up with "something that looked like an iceberg version of Gotham City with water running through it." They created a basic model of a glacier and then designers created a program that added elements like roads, intersections and ravines until they had a complex, yet organic-looking, cityscape. For the Paris-folding sequence, Franklin had artists producing concept sketches and then they created rough computer animations to give them an idea of what the sequence looked like while in motion. Later during principal photography, Nolan was able to direct Leonardo DiCaprio and Ellen Page based on this rough computer animation Franklin had created. *Inception* had close to 500 visual effects shots (in comparison, *Batman Begins* had approximately 620) which is considered minor in comparison to contemporary visual effects epics that can have around 1,500 or 2,000 VFX shots.

Music

Inception: Music from the Motion Picture	
Film score by Hans Zimmer	
Released	July 13, 2010
Genre	Soundtrack
Length	49:13
Label	Reprise
Hans Zimmer chronology	
Henry IV (2010)	*Inception* (2010)

Hans Zimmer scored the film, marking his third collaboration with Nolan following *Batman Begins* and *The Dark Knight*. According to Zimmer, it's "a very electronic score". Nolan asked Zimmer to compose and finish the score as he was shooting the film. The composer said, "He wanted to unleash my imagination in the best possible way". At one point, while composing the score, Zimmer incorporated a guitar sound reminiscent of Ennio Morricone and was interested in having Johnny Marr, former guitarist in the influential 80s rock band, The Smiths, play these parts. He asked Nolan, who agreed and then Zimmer approached Marr who accepted his offer. Marr spent four 12-hour days working on the score, playing notes written by Zimmer with a 12-string guitar.

For inspiration, Zimmer read *Gödel, Escher, Bach: An Eternal Golden Braid* by Douglas Hofstadter because it combined "the idea of playfulness in mathematics and playfulness in music". Zimmer did not assemble a temp score but "every now and then they would call and say 'we need a little something here.' But that was OK because much of the music pieces aren't that scene specific. They fall into little categories". While writing the screenplay, Nolan wrote in Édith Piaf's "Non, je ne regrette rien" but almost took it out when he cast Marion Cotillard, who had just completed an Oscar-winning turn as Piaf in the 2007 film *La Vie en rose*. Zimmer convinced Nolan to keep it in the film and also integrated elements of the song into his score.

The trailers for the film feature specially composed music by Zack Hemsey, which does not appear on the official soundtrack.[citation needed]

Track listing

All tracks written and composed by Hans Zimmer.

No.	Title	Length
	Inception: Music from the Motion Picture	
1.	"Half Remembered Dream"	1:12
2.	"We Built Our Own World"	1:55
3.	"Dream Is Collapsing"	2:28
4.	"Radical Notion"	3:43
5.	"Old Souls"	7:44
6.	"528491"	2:23
7.	"Mombasa"	4:54
8.	"One Simple Idea"	2:28
9.	"Dream Within a Dream"	5:04
10.	"Waiting for a Train"	9:30
11.	"Paradox"	3:25
12.	"Time"	4:35
13.	"Projections (Bonus Track)"	7:04
14.	"Don't Think About Elephants (Bonus Track)"	5:35

Marketing

In the spring of 2010, a viral marketing campaign was started for the film. On June 2, 2010, a manual was sent out to various companies. The manual was filled with bizarre images and text all relating to *Inception*. As the month went on, more and more viral marketing began to surface, including posters, ads, phone applications, and strange websites all related to the film. On June 7, 2010, a behind the scenes featurette on the film was released in HD on Yahoo! Movies. Warner Bros. has spent $100 million marketing the film.

Release

Inception was released in both conventional and IMAX theaters on July 16, 2010. The film had its world premiere at Leicester Square in London, England on July 8, 2010.

Critical response

Many critics have applauded what they saw as a smart and innovative story, as well as the cast, score, and memorable action scenes. Review aggregate Rotten Tomatoes reports that 87% of critics have given the film a positive review based on 258 reviews, with an average score of 8/10. Among Rotten Tomatoes' *Top Critics*, which consists of popular and notable critics from the top newspapers, websites, television and radio programs, the film holds an overall approval rating of 79%, based on a sample of 38 reviews. The website reported the critical consensus, "Smart, innovative, and thrilling, *Inception*

Producer Emma Thomas and director Christopher Nolan at a panel for the film at WonderCon in April 2010

is that rare summer blockbuster that succeeds viscerally as well as intellectually." Review aggregator Metacritic assigned the film a weighted average score of 74 based on 42 reviews from mainstream critics, considered to be "Generally favorable reviews." CinemaScore polls conducted during the opening weekend revealed the average grade cinemagoers gave *Inception* was B+ on an A+ to F scale.

Rolling Stone magazine's Peter Travers gave *Inception* its first positive notice, calling it a "wildly ingenious chess game," and added "the result is a knockout." In his review for *Variety*, Justin Chang praised the film as "a conceptual tour de force" and wrote, "applying a vivid sense of procedural detail to a fiendishly intricate yarn set in the labyrinth of the unconscious mind, the writer-director has devised a heist thriller for surrealists, a Jungian's *Rififi*, that challenges viewers to sift through multiple layers of (un)reality." Jim Vejvoda of *IGN* rated the film perfect, deeming it "a singular accomplishment from a filmmaker who has only gotten better with each film." Relevant Magazine's David Roark called it Nolan's greatest accomplishment, saying, "Visually, intellectually and emotionally, Inception is a masterpiece."

Empire magazine rated it five stars in the August 2010 issue and wrote, "it feels like Stanley Kubrick adapting the work of the great sci-fi author William Gibson ... Nolan delivers another true original: welcome to an undiscovered country." *Entertainment Weekly* gave the film a B+ rating and Lisa Schwarzbaum wrote, "It's a rolling explosion of images as hypnotizing and sharply angled as any in a drawing by M.C. Escher or a state-of-the-biz videogame; the backwards splicing of Nolan's own *Memento* looks rudimentary by comparison." *The New York Post* gave the film a four star rating and Lou Lumenick wrote, "DiCaprio, who has never been better as the tortured hero, draws you in with a love story that will appeal even to non-sci-fi fans." Roger Ebert of the *Chicago Sun-Times* awarded the film a perfect four stars and said that *Inception* "is all about process, about fighting our way through enveloping sheets of reality and dream, reality within dreams, dreams without reality. It's a breathtaking juggling act." Richard Roeper, also of *The Chicago Sun-Times*, gave *Inception* a perfect score of "A+" and noted that it is "one of the best movies of the [21st] century."

In his review for the *Chicago Tribune*, Michael Phillips gave the film 3 stars out of 4 and wrote, "I found myself wishing *Inception* were weirder, further out ... the film is Nolan's labyrinth all the way, and it's gratifying to experience a summer movie with large visual ambitions and with nothing more or less on its mind than (as Shakespeare said) a dream that hath no bottom." *Time* magazine's Richard Corliss wrote the film's "noble intent is to implant one man's vision in the mind of a vast audience ... The idea of moviegoing as communal dreaming is a century old. With *Inception*, viewers have a chance to see that notion get a state-of-the-art update." *Los Angeles Times*' Kenneth Turan felt that Nolan was able to blend "the best of traditional and modern filmmaking. If you're searching for smart and nervy popular entertainment, this is what it looks like." *USA Today* rated the film three-and-a-half stars out of four and Claudia Puig felt that Nolan "regards his viewers as possibly smarter than they are—or at least as capable of rising to his inventive level. That's a tall order. But it's refreshing to find a director who makes us stretch, even occasionally struggle, to keep up."

Not all reviewers, however, were so positive about the film. *New York* magazine's David Edelstein was reported to "have no idea what so many people are raving about. It's as if someone went into their heads while they were sleeping and planted the idea that *Inception* is a visionary masterpiece and—hold on ... Whoa! I think I get it. The movie is a metaphor for the power of delusional hype—a metaphor for itself." Rex Reed of *The New York Observer* explained the film's development as "pretty much what we've come to expect from summer movies in general and Christopher Nolan movies in particular ... [it] doesn't seem like much of an accomplishment to me." A.O. Scott of *The New York Times* commented "there is a lot to see in *Inception*, there is nothing that counts as genuine vision. Mr. Nolan's idea of the mind is too literal, too logical, too rule-bound to allow the full measure of madness."

Box office

See also: List of highest-grossing films

In the United States and Canada, *Inception* was released theatrically in 3,792 conventional theaters and 195 IMAX theaters. The film grossed $23.7 million during its opening day on July 16, 2010, with midnight screenings in 1,500 locations. Overall the film made $62.7 million and debuted at #1 on its opening weekend. *Inception*'s opening weekend gross made it the second highest-grossing debut for a stand-alone science-fiction film, falling behind *Avatar*'s $77 million opening weekend gross in 2009. In its second and third weekends the film held the top spot with drops of just 32% ($42.7 million) and 36% ($27.5 million) respectively. In its fourth week of release, the film fell to the second spot to *The Other Guys*.

As of October 10, 2010, *Inception* has grossed an estimated $289,201,000 in the United States and Canada and an estimated $515,000,000 overseas. In total, the film has grossed $804,201,000 worldwide thus far. It is the second-highest-grossing Christopher Nolan movie in the U.S. and Canada, behind *The Dark Knight* which grossed $533 million, the highest-grossing one overseas, surpassing *The Dark Knight*, which grossed $469 million, and the second highest-grossing one worldwide behind *The Dark Knight* (which grossed $1.002 billion overall). It is the third 2010 film that reaches the $800-million mark, while, in overseas earnings, it is the third picture of 2010 that crosses the $500-million mark.

It became the highest-grossing *Crime time*, *Heist/caper* and *Mindbender* movie ever at the North American box office. In these territories, it is also the fifth highest-grossing film of 2010. Internationally, it became the third-highest-grossing 2010 release behind *Toy Story 3* and *Alice in Wonderland* and it is currently the 26th highest grossing film of all time.

References

Bibliography

- *Inception Production Notes*, (2010, Warner Brothers). [1] Retrieved on September 4, 2010. .

Further reading

- "How To Understand Inception, In One Easy Chart" [2].
- Neurosecurity
- "The Influences of *Inception*" [3].
- "Interview: *Inception* Cinematographer Wally Pfister" [4].
- "With *Inception*, Can Christopher Nolan Save the Summer?" [5].
- "An Illustrated Guide To The 5 Levels Of *Inception*" [6].
- "Everything you wanted to know about *Inception*" [7]. *Salon*.
- Nina Shen Rastogi (July 20, 2010). "Five Ways of Looking at Inception" [8]. Summary of different interpretations of the film

External links

- Official website [9]
- *Inception* [10] at the Internet Movie Database
- *Inception* [11] at Allmovie
- *Inception* [12] at Rotten Tomatoes
- *Inception* [13] at Metacritic
- *Inception* [14] at Box Office Mojo

Awards and Recognitions

American Film Institute

American Film Institute	
Established	1967
Location	Los Angeles, CA
Website	www.AFI.com [1]

The **American Film Institute** is an independent non-profit organization created by the National Endowment for the Arts, which was established in 1967 when President Lyndon B. Johnson signed the National Foundation on the Arts and the Humanities Act. The organization describes itself as "a national institute providing leadership in screen education and the recognition and celebration of excellence in the art of film, television and digital media."

The AFI Conservatory focuses on training through hands-on experience with established artists.

The American Film Institute re-opened the AFI Silver theatre in Silver Spring, Maryland, near Washington, D.C., in April 2003.

History

The American Film Institute was founded in 1967 as a national arts organization to preserve the legacy of America's film heritage, educate the next generation of filmmakers and honor the artists and their work. The National Endowment for the Arts and Humanities recommended creating AFI "to enrich and nurture the art of film in America" with initial funding from the National Endowment for the Arts, the Motion Picture Association of America and the Ford Foundation. The original 22-member Board of Trustees included Chair Gregory Peck and Vice Chair Sidney Poitier as well as Francis Ford Coppola, Arthur Schlesinger, Jr., Jack Valenti and other representatives from the arts and academia.

George Stevens, Jr., was the founding director. Jean Picker Firstenberg was President and CEO from 1980 to 2007. Bob Gazzale was named President and CEO in 2007. As a national nonprofit organization, the institute funds its efforts through contributions and sponsorships from large corporations and small companies, donations from individuals and its AFI membership program.

AFI Conservatory

The AFI Conservatory describes itself as a "world-renowned Conservatory where a dedicated group of working professionals from the film and television communities serve as mentors in a hands-on, production-based environment nurturing the talents of tomorrow's storytellers." In a two-year program that emphasizes narrative storytelling and grants an MFA, Fellows specialize in one of six disciplines: Cinematography, Directing, Editing, Production Design, Producing and Screenwriting.

In 1969, the institute established the Center for Advanced Film Studies at Greystone, the Doheny Mansion in Beverly Hills, CA. The first class included filmmakers Terrence Malick, David Lynch, Caleb Deschanel and Paul Schrader. That program grew into the AFI Conservatory, a fully accredited graduate film school, located in the hills above Hollywood, CA. In addition to the Conservatory, AFI has a tuition-free program called the AFI Directing Workshop for Women that operates each spring and summer from the Los Angeles campus.

Notable alumni

Several AFI Alums have received both national and international recognition. Among the notable alumni of AFI are: Darren Aronofsky, Jon Avnet, Keith D. Black, Stuart Cornfeld, Bill Duke, Edward James Olmos, , Todd Field, Rodrigo Garcia, Anne Garefino, Steve Golin, Amy Heckerling, Marshall Herskovitz, Janusz Kamiński, Mimi Leder, David Lynch, Terrence Malick, John McTiernan, Paul Schrader, Frank Spotnitz, Mark Waters, Gary Winick, Ed Zwick, and Susannah Grant.

AFI Programs

AFI Catalog Of Feature Films

The AFI Catalog of Feature Films, started in 1968, is an online database that preserves the history of American film in authoritative, encyclopedic detail. A prime research tool for film historians, the catalog consists of entries on more than 50,000 films, from 1893 to the mid-1970s, documenting casts, crews, synopses and production notes. New catalog entries of the remaining 15,000 American feature films produced between 1974 and present day are incorporated every year.

AFI Life Achievement Award

Main article: AFI Life Achievement Award

AFI Awards

The annual AFI Awards honors the creative ensembles of the 10 outstanding movies and television shows of the year. Two 13-person juries composed of artists, academics, critics and AFI Trustees deliberate, discuss and determine the honored ensembles, who are then feted at a private event in

January. In addition, Ten Moments of Significance, documenting the year's media milestones, are entered into an ongoing almanac.

AFI 100 Years... series

The popular AFI 100 Years... series, which ran from 1998 to 2008, and created jury-selected lists of America's best movies in categories including Musicals, Laughs and Thrills, drove new generations to experience classic American films. The juries consisted of over 1,500 artists, scholars, critics and historians, with movies selected based on the film's popularity over time, historical significance and cultural impact. *Citizen Kane* was voted the greatest American film twice.

AFI Film Festivals

AFI operates two film festivals: AFI FEST in Los Angeles, CA, and AFI-Discovery Channel SILVERDOCS documentary festival in Silver Spring, MD. AFI FEST is the only film festival in the US to hold FIAPF (Fédération Internationale des Associations de Producteurs de Films) accreditation.

AFI Silver Theatre and Cultural Center

As the largest nonprofit exhibitor in the United States, AFI screens films regularly at the AFI Silver Theatre and Cultural Center in Silver Spring, MD, and the ArcLight Cinemas and Skirball Cultural Center in Los Angeles, CA. Programming at the AFI Silver Theatre consists of an eclectic mix of retrospectives, festivals and first-run features as well as community events and educational activities.

AFI Digital Content Lab

The AFI Digital Content Lab is a research and development facility for digital media located on the LA campus. The lab explores and creates digital entertainment prototypes for film, television, video games, broadband and mobile phones.

AFI ScreenNation

AFI ScreenNation is a Web site featuring AFI-produced educational materials and tips for new filmmakers to share work, receive recognition and compete for prizes.

References

- Official website [2]
- AFI Fest Official website [3]
- AFI Los Angeles Film Festival - History and Information [4]

International Film Festival Rotterdam

International Film Festival Rotterdam	
The festival logo	
Location	Rotterdam, Netherlands
Official website [1]	

The **International Film Festival Rotterdam** (**IFFR**) is an annual film festival held in various cinemas in Rotterdam, Netherlands at the end of January. It is one of the larger film festivals in Europe, arguably in the *Big Five*, alongside Cannes, Venice, Berlin, and Locarno. Ever since the beginning of the festival in 1972, the symbol of the IFFR has been a tiger, loosely based on the M.G.M. lion.

Festival

The International Film Festival Rotterdam puts its emphasis not only on an impressively diverse programme but on building relationships with and between film-makers and audiences.

Rather than red-carpet events, it encourages film makers to mingle with the crowds, giving the event a unique atmosphere and a fiercely loyal following locally and internationally - around 90% of tickets are sold to regular supporters.

The festival then has a serious commitment to film lovers and film making - screenings are shown without 'popcorn breaks', trailers or other commercials. This sense of purpose plays a crucial role in attracting the best directors to the event, allowing it to forge a reputation for diversity, discovery and innovation.

History

The first festival—then called 'Film International' -- was organized in June 1972 under the inspired leadership of Huub Bals. From the beginning, the festival has profiled itself as a promotor of alternative, innovative and non-commercial films, with an emphasis on the Far East and developing countries. Despite financial difficulties in the mid-1980s, the festival has grown steadily, reaching 353,000 visitors in 2010.

After the festival founder's sudden death in 1988, a fund was initiated and named after him (Hubert Bals Fund), used for supporting filmmakers from developing countries.

The non-competitive character of the festival changed in 1995, when the *VPRO Tiger Awards* were introduced—three yearly prizes for young filmmakers making their first or second film. The next year, Simon Field, formerly Cinema Director at the London Institute of Contemporary Arts, became director of the festival. In 2004 Sandra den Hamer took over as director of the festival, and since 1st September 2007, the leadership is in the hands of Rutger Wolfson.

Rutger Wolfson Director of the Film Festival Rotterdam

Festival Screening locations

The Pathé cinema at Schouwburgplein

The Pathé cinema at Schouwburgplein is one of the biggest cinemas in the country and boasts the largest screen in the Netherlands. The modern edifice − located between the Schouwburg and De Doelen − is dramatically lit by night, dominating the square.

De Doelen

De Doelen is the Central Box office during the festival

Cinerama

Cinerama is a magnificent old cinema with 7 theaters and more than 1000 seats. You can wait for your film at the well-stocked reading table or enjoy a nice drink in the comfortable lounge.

WORM

Worm is the main venue for the Starting from Scratch activities with film screenings, performances, installations, the Metamkine workshop, the Scratching from Start party and meeting point for activities in the lab of WORM.filmwerkplaats

Old Luxor Theater

The Old Luxor Theater dates back to 1917 and is a "Grand Dame" amongst Rotterdam theaters. It has been thoroughly renovated multiple times, but retains an atmosphere that lends a special touch to the cinematic experience.

De Rotterdamse Schouwburg

The Rotterdam Schouwburg is located in the heart of Rotterdam, on the famous Schouwburgplein. It is one of the main performing arts centers of the city, offering a wide range of critically acclaimed dance, opera and theatrical performances.

VPRO Tiger Award winners

Year	Film	Director	Country of origin
1995	*Postman*	He Jianjun	China
	Fuyu no kappa	Kazama Shiori	Japan
	Thalassa, Thalassa, Ruckkehr Zum Mmer	Bogdan Dumitrescu	Germany/Romania
1996	*Sons*	Zhang Yuan	China
	Like Grains of Sand	Hasiguchi Ryosuke	Japan
	Small Faces	Gillies MacKinnon	United Kingdom
1997	*Last Holiday*	Amir Karakulov	Kazakhstan
	The Day a Pig Fell into the Well	Hung Sang-soo	South Korea
	Robinson in Space	Patrick Keiller	United Kingdom

1998	Buttoners	Petr Zelenka	Czech Republic
	Giro di lune tra terra e mare	Giuseppe Gaudino	Italy
	Die Siebtelbauern	Stefan Ruzowitzky	Austria
1999	The Iron Heel of Oligarchy	Alexander Bashirov	Russia
	Plus Qu'hier, Moins Que Demain	Laurent Achard	France
	Following	Christopher Nolan	United Kingdom
2000	Suzhou River	Lou Ye	China
	Mundo Grúa	Pablo Trapero	Argentina
	Bye Bye Blue Bird	Katrin Ottarsdottír	Denmark
2001	Bad Company	Furumaya Tomoyuki	Japan
	The Days Between	Maria Speth	Germany
	25 Watts	Juan Pablo Rebella & Pablo Stoll	Uruguay
2002	Tussenland	Eugenie Jansen	The Netherlands
	Everyday God Kisses Us on the Mouth	Siniṣa Dragin	Romania
	Wild Bees	Bohdan Sláma	Czech Republic
2003	With Love. Lilya	Larisa Sadilova	Russia
	Extraño	Santiago Loza	Argentina
	Jealousy Is My Middle Name	Park Chan-ok	South Korea
2004	The Missing	Lee Kang-sheng	Taiwan
	Summer in the Golden Valley	Srđan Vuletić	Bosnia-Herzegovina
	En Route	Jan Krüger	Germany
2005	Changing Destiny	Daniele Gaglianone	Italy
	4	Ilya Khrzhanovsky	Russia
	The Sky Turns	Mercedes Alvarez	Spain
2006	Walking on the Wild Side	Han Jie	China
	The Dog Pound	Manuel Nieto Zas	Uruguay/Argentina/Canada/Spain
	Old Joy	Kelly Reichardt	United States of America
2007	Love Conquers All	Tan Chui Mui	Malaysia
	The Unpolished	Pia Marais	Germany
	Bog of Beasts	Claudio Assis	Brazil
	AFR (ex aequo)	Morten Hartz Kaplers	Denmark

2008	Go With Peace Jamil	Omar Shargawi	Denmark
	Wonderful Town	Aditya Assarat	Thailand
	Flower in the Pocket	Liew Seng Tat	Malaysia
2009	Be Calm and Count to Seven	Ramtin Lavafipour	Iran
	Breathless	Yang Ik-June	South Korea
	Wrong Rosary	Mahmut Fazil Coskun	Turkey

External links

- International Film Festival Rotterdam [1] (official website)
- New Arrivals [2]
- Hubert Bals Fund [3]
- youtube channel [4]

Broadcast Film Critics Association Award

The **Broadcast Film Critics Association Awards**, commonly called the **Critics' Choice Awards**, are bestowed annually by the Broadcast Film Critics Association to honor the finest in cinematic achievement. Nominees are selected by written ballots in a week-long voting period, and are announced in December. The winners are revealed at the annual Critics' Choice Awards ceremony in January. The awards are currently broadcast live on the VH1 television network.. The 2007 and 2008 Awards were at the Santa Monica Civic Auditorium, the 2009 event -- renamed The Critics' Choice Movie Awards - is being held at the refurbished historic Hollywood Palladium on January 15. Special awards are given out at the discretion of the BFCA Board of Directors.

The Broadcast Film Critics Association prides itself on its ability to anticipate Academy Award nominations: between 1997 and 2004, the Critics' Choice nominations predicted all but two of 35 Academy Award nominations for Best Picture. By comparison, the Golden Globe Awards were three times more likely to differ during the same period.[citation needed] However, the fact that the BFCA — which typically nominates nine or ten films for Best Film — chooses more than the five nominations of the Academy Awards and Golden Globes may account for some of this greater predictive power. The nominations for the 2010 Awards were announced on December 14, 2009.

For yearly results, see Category:Broadcast Film Critics Association Awards.

External links

- Broadcast Film Critics Association website [1]

Independent Spirit Awards

Film Independent's Spirit Awards	
Awarded for	Best in independent films
Presented by	Film Independent
Country	United States
First awarded	1984
Official website	http://spiritawards.com/

The **Independent Spirit Awards** (originally known as the **FINDIE or Friends of Independents Awards**), founded in 1984, are awards dedicated to independent filmmakers. Winners were typically presented with acrylic glass pyramids containing suspended shoestrings representing the paltry budgets of independent films. In 1986, the event was renamed the Independent Spirit Awards. The Independent Spirit Awards are presented by Film Independent, a non-profit organization dedicated to independent film and independent filmmakers. In 2007, the ceremony was slightly changed to **Film Independent's Spirit Awards**. Since 2006, winners have received a trophy depicting a bird sitting atop of a pole with the shoestrings from the previous design wrapped around the pole.

The awards show was previously held inside a tent on the beach in Santa Monica, California, usually on the day before the Academy Awards (since 1999; originally the Saturday before). Since 1994, the show has been broadcast on the Independent Film Channel.

The 2009 awards took place on February 21, 2009. Independent Spirit Awards 2010 were held on March 5, 2010 inside a tent in downtown Los Angeles.

Categories

- Best Film
- Best Director
- Best First Feature
- Independent Spirit Award for Best Lead Female
- Independent Spirit Award for Best Male Lead
- Independent Spirit Award for Best Supporting Female
- Independent Spirit Award for Best Supporting Male
- Best Screenplay
- Best First Screenplay
- Best Foreign Film
- Best Documentary Feature
- Best Cinematography
- John Cassavetes Award
- Robert Altman Award
- Acura Someone to Watch Award
- Piaget Producers Award
- Truer than Fiction Award

External links

- Official website [1]
- Film Independent [2]
- Independent Spirit Awards [3] at Internet Movie Database

Sundance Film Festival

Sundance Film Festival	

Location	Park City, Utah, USA
Language	International
Official website [1]	

The **Sundance Film Festival** is a film festival that takes place annually in the state of Utah, in the United States. It is the largest independent cinema festival in the United States. Held in January in Park City, Salt Lake City, and Ogden, as well as the Sundance Resort, the festival is the premier showcase for new work from American and international independent filmmakers. The festival comprises competitive sections for American and international dramatic and documentary films, both feature-length films and short films, and a group of non-competitive showcase sections, including the New Frontier, Spectrum, and Park City @ Midnight.

History

Utah/US Film Festival

Sundance began in Salt Lake City in 1978 as the Utah/US Film Festival in an effort to attract more filmmakers to Utah. It was founded by Sterling Van Wagenen (then head of Wildwood, Robert Redford's company), John Earle and Cirina Hampton Catania (both serving on the Utah Film Commission at the time).

With Chairperson Robert Redford, and the help of Governor Scott Matheson of Utah, the goal of the festival was to showcase strictly American-made films, highlight what the potential of independent film could be and to increase visibility for filmmaking in Utah. At the time, the main focus of the event was to conduct a competition for independent American films, present a series of retrospective films and filmmaker panel discussions and to celebrate the Frank Capra Award (given the first year to Jimmy Stewart); it highlighted the work of "regional" filmmakers who worked outside the Hollywood system.

The jury of the 1978 festival was headed by Gary Allison, and included Verna Fields, Linwood Gale Dunn, Katherine Ross, Charles E. Sellier Jr., Mark Rydell, and Anthea Sylbert.

In 1979, Sterling Van Wagenen left to head up the first year "pilot" program of what was to become the Sundance Institute and Cirina Hampton Catania took over as Executive Director of the Festival. Over 60 films were screened at the Festival that year, the Frank Capra Award went to Jimmy Stewart and panels featured many well-known Hollywood filmmakers. The Festival made a profit for the first time. In 1980, Catania left the Festival to pursue a production career in Hollywood.

Several factors helped propel the growth of Utah/US Film Festival. First was the involvement of actor Robert Redford. Redford, a Utah resident, became the festival's inaugural chairman and having his name associated with Sundance gave the festival great attention. Secondly, the country was hungry for a venue that would celebrate American-made films as the only other festival doing so at the time was the then fledgling Dallas Film Fest. Response in Hollywood was unprecedented as major studios did all they could to contribute their resources.

In 1981, the festival moved to Park City, Utah and changed from September to January. The move from late summer to mid-winter was reportedly done on the advice of Hollywood director Sydney Pollack, who suggested that running a film festival in a ski resort during winter would draw more attention from Hollywood.

In 1984-85, the now well-established Sundance Institute, headed by Sterling Van Wagenen, took over management of the US Film Festival and changed the name to Sundance. Gary Beer and Sterling Van Wagenen spearheaded production of the inaugural Sundance Film Festival which included Program Director Tony Safford and Administrative Director Jenny Walz Selby.

Sundance Institute

Management of the Festival was taken over by the Sundance Institute, a non-profit organization, in 1985. In 1991 the Festival was officially renamed the *Sundance Film Festival*, after Redford's character The Sundance Kid from the movie *Butch Cassidy and the Sundance Kid*.

From 2006 through 2008, the Sundance Institute collaborated with the Brooklyn Academy of Music (BAM) on a special series of film screenings, performances, panel discussions, and special events bringing the institute's activities and the festival's programming to New York City.

Notability of Festivals

Many famous independent filmmakers received their big break at Sundance, including Kevin Smith, Robert Rodriguez, Quentin Tarantino, Paul Thomas Anderson, Steven Soderbergh, James Wan, Edward Burns and Jim Jarmusch. It is also responsible for bringing wider attention to films such as *Saw*, *Garden State*, *Super Troopers*, *The Blair Witch Project*, *Better Luck Tomorrow*, *Primer*, *Reservoir Dogs*, *Little Miss Sunshine*, *El Mariachi*, *Moon*, *Clerks*, *Thank You for Smoking*, *sex, lies, and videotape*, *The Brothers McMullen* and *Napoleon Dynamite*.

Three Seasons was the first in Festival history to ever receive both the Grand Jury Award and Audience Award in 1999. Later films which also won both awards are: *God Grew Tired of Us* in 2006 (documentary category), *Quinceañera* in 2006 (dramatic category), and *Precious* in 2009.

In January 2009, the festival was marked by an early exodus of celebrities who turned up for the first few days of the festival, but left early to attend the inauguration of the first African-American US President, Barack Obama, in Washington, D.C., on Tuesday, January 20, 2009.

Growth of the festival

The Festival has changed over the decades from a low-profile venue for small-budget, independent creators from outside the Hollywood system to a media extravaganza for Hollywood celebrity actors, paparazzi, and luxury lounges set up by companies that are not affiliated with Sundance, though the Festival itself has tried to curb these activities in recent years, beginning in 2007 with their ongoing "Focus On Film" campaign.

In 2010, a slew of changes were made to the Sundance Film Festival. Some of the changes made in 2010 include: a new programming category called "NEXT" for extremely low-budget films, and the Sundance Film Festival U.S.A. program, in which eight of the festival's films will be shown in eight theaters around the country.

Directors

- John Cooper - March 2009
- Geoff Gilmore - 1991-2009

In popular culture

In August 1998, the animated television series *South Park* episode "Chef's Chocolate Salty Balls" depicts the directors of the Sundance Festival moving it to a "different small mountain town", that of the show's main setting South Park, in order to "drain it and morph it into a new LA".

In the television series *Entourage*, one of the independent movies which Vincent Chase stars in (*Queens Boulevard*) premieres at the Sundance Film Festival, where it begins its gains in popularity.

In animated television series *The Simpsons* episode "Any Given Sundance", Lisa Simpson enters a documentary about her family into the Sundance Film Festival.

See also

- List of Sundance Film Festival award winners
- List of Sundance Film Festival selections
- Sundance Channel
- Sundance Institute
- TRe-ChE ShOrt FeSt '09 Internacional [2]

References

Further reading

- *Down and Dirty Pictures: Miramax, Sundance, and the Rise of Independent Film* by Peter Biskind (Simon & Schuster, 2004)
- *Party in a Box: The Story of the Sundance Film Festival* by Lory Smith (Gibbs Smith Publishers, 1999)
- *Sundance - A Festival Virgin's Guide* by Benjamin Craig (Cinemagine Media Publishing, 2004)
- *Sundancing: Hanging Out And Listening In At America's Most Important Film Festival* by John Anderson (Harper Paperbacks, 2000)

External links

- Official website [3]
- Sundance - A Festival Virgin's Guide [4] - detailed festival history and information for attendees.
- Festival Guide [5] - Indie film resource
- LA Times article on 2010 competition films [6]

Press

- Photos from Sundance Film Festival 2010 [7] (January 26, 2010)

Saturn Award

Saturn Award	
The Saturn Award	
Awarded for	Best in science fiction, fantasy and horror film and television
Presented by	Academy of Science Fiction, Fantasy & Horror Films
Country	United States
First awarded	1972
Official website	http://www.saturnawards.org/

The **Saturn Award** is an award presented annually by the **Academy of Science Fiction, Fantasy & Horror Films** to honor the top works in science fiction, fantasy, and horror in film, television, and home video. The Saturn Awards were devised by Dr. Donald A. Reed in 1972, who felt that films within those genres were never given the appreciation they deserved at that time. The physical award is a representation of the planet Saturn, surrounded with a ring of film. The award was initially and is still sometimes loosely referred to as a **Golden Scroll**.

Similar to other awards, like the Oscars, the Emmys and the Grammys, the Saturn Awards are voted on by members of the presenting Academy. There are also special awards for lifetime achievement in the field.

The awards were first presented in 1972 by William Shatner, well-known as Captain James T. Kirk in the hit TV show *Star Trek*.

Although the awards still primarily nominate films and TV in the science fiction, fantasy and horror categories, the Saturns have also begun to recognize productions in standard dramatic genres as well. The 35th annual awards, to be presented in 2009, for example, includes nominations for films ranging from the 1940s wartime classic *Casablanca* to the 2008 film *Slumdog Millionaire*.

Award categories

Motion picture

- Best Science Fiction Film
- Best Fantasy Film
- Best Horror Film
- Best Action/Adventure/Thriller Film
- Best Animated Film
- Best International Film
- Best Direction
- Best Actor
- Best Actress
- Best Supporting Actor
- Best Supporting Actress
- Best Performance by a Younger Actor
- Best Writing
- Best Music
- Best Make-up
- Best Costume
- Best Special Effects
- Best Production Design

In addition there was an Award for Best Foreign Film in 1980. The only winner in that category was Dinner for Adele (1977).

Television

- Best Network Television Series
- Best Syndicated/Cable Television Series
- Best Television Presentation
- Best Actor on Television
- Best Actress on Television
- Best Supporting Actor on Television
- Best Supporting Actress on Television
- Best International Series

Home video

- Best DVD Release
- Best DVD Special Edition Release
- Best DVD Classic Film Release
- Best DVD Collection
- Best DVD Television Release

Year-By-Year results

- **2003:** 30th Saturn Awards
- **2004:** 31st Saturn Awards
- **2005:** 32nd Saturn Awards
- **2006:** 33rd Saturn Awards
- **2007:** 34th Saturn Awards
- **2008:** 35th Saturn Awards
- **2009:** 36th Saturn Awards

See also

- Hugo Award
- Scream Awards

External links

- The Official Saturn Awards Site [1]
- The most-honored films nominated for a Saturn Award [2]
- Saturn Awards on IMDb [3]
- William Shatner in an infamous appearance at the 1978 Saturn Awards [4]
- Saturn Awards 2009 at FEARnet [5]

Empire Awards

Since 1995, *Empire*—Britain's biggest selling film magazine—has organised the annual **Empire Movie Awards**. They were sponsored by Sony Ericsson until 2009 and are now sponsored by Jameson. The awards are voted for by readers of the magazine.

Award categories

The categories for awards are:

- Best British Actor
- Best British Actress
- Best British Film
- Best Debut (until 2002)
- Best Newcomer (beginning 2003)
- Best Actor
- Best Actress
- Best Director
- Best Film
- Empire Lifetime Achievement Award (until 2003)
- Empire Career Achievement Award (2004)
- Best British Director (1997–2001)
- Empire Inspiration Award (1997, 1999, 2001, 2002, 2010)
- Empire Movie Masterpiece (1999, 2000)
- Special Award for Contribution to Cinema (2000)
- Empire Independent Spirit Award (beginning 2002)
- Sony Ericsson Best Scene (beginning 2003)
- Done in 60 Seconds (beginning 2008)

1998 Winners and Nominees

Best Actor

Tom Hanks - Saving Private Ryan

- *Matt Damon - Good Will Hunting*
- *Jim Carrey - The Truman Show*
- *Samuel L. Jackson - Jackie Brown*
- *Jeff Bridges - The Big Lebowski*

Best Actress

Cate Blanchett - Elizabeth

- *Helen Hunt - As Good as It Gets*
- *Jennifer Lopez - Out of Sight*
- *Gwyneth Paltrow - Sliding Doors*
- *Pam Grier - Jackie Brown*

Best British Actor

Peter Mullan - My Name Is Joe

- *Ewan McGregor - Velvet Goldmine*
- *Bob Hoskins - 24/7*
- *Joseph Fiennes - Elizabeth*
- *Gary Oldman - Lost in Space*

Best British Actress

Kate Winslet - Titanic

- *Minnie Driver - Good Will Hunting*
- *Catherine Zeta-Jones - Zorro*
- *Emily Watson - The Boxer*
- *Anna Friel - The Land Girls*

Best British Director

Peter Howitt - Sliding Doors

- *Shane Meadows - 24/7*
- *Guy Ritchie - Lock, Stock and Two Smoking Barrels*
- *Nick Hamm - Martha*
- *Ken Loach - My Name Is Joe*

Best Director

Steven Spielberg - Saving Private Ryan

- *Peter Weir - The Truman Show*
- *James Cameron - Titanic*
- *Steven Soderbergh - Out of Sight*
- *Ang Lee - The Ice Storm*

Best Newcomer

Vinnie Jones - Lock, Stock and Two Smoking Barrels

* Cate Blanchett - Elizabeth
* Charlize Theron - The Devil's Advocate
* Denise Richards - Starship Troopers
* Shane Meadows - 24/7

Best British Film

Lock, Stock and Two Smoking Barrels

* Elizabeth
* Sliding Doors
* My Name Is Joe
* 24/7

Best Film

Titanic

* Saving Private Ryan
* The Truman Show
* The Big Lebowski
* Good Will Hunting

Lifetime Achievement Award

Bob Hoskins

1999 Winners

* Best Actor

Pierce Brosnan - The World Is Not Enough

* Best Actress

Gwyneth Paltrow - Shakespeare in Love

* Best British Actor

Hugh Grant - Notting Hill

* Best British Actress

Helena Bonham Carter - Fight Club

* Best British Director

Roger Mitchell - Notting Hill

- *Best British Film*

Notting Hill

- *Best Director*

M. Night Shyamalan - The Sixth Sense

- *Best Film*

The Matrix

- *Best Newcomer*

Carrie-Anne Moss - The Matrix, East Is East

2000 Winners and Nominees

Best Actor

Russell Crowe - Gladiator

- *Kevin Spacey - American Beauty*
- *George Clooney - O Brother, Where Art Thou?*
- *Jim Carrey - How the Grinch Stole Christmas*
- *John Cusack - High Fidelity*

Best Actress

Connie Nielsen - Gladiator

- *Hilary Swank - Boys Don't Cry*
- *Kate Winslet - Quills*
- *Julia Roberts - Erin Brockovich*
- *Angelina Jolie - Girl, Interrupted*

Best British Actor

Vinnie Jones - Snatch

- *Jude Law - The Talented Mr. Ripley*
- *Christian Bale - American Psycho*
- *Michael Caine - The Cider House Rules*
- *Robert Carlyle - Angela's Ashes*

Best British Actress

Julie Walters - Billy Elliot

- *Kathy Burke - Kevin & Perry Go Large*
- *Thandie Newton - Mission: Impossible II*
- *Brenda Blethyn - Saving Grace*
- *Samantha Morton - Sweet and Lowdown*

Best British Director

Guy Ritchie - Snatch

- *Sam Mendes - American Beauty*
- *Stephen Daldry - Billy Elliot*
- *Ridley Scott - Gladiator*
- *Nick Park and Peter Lord - Chicken Run*

Best British Film

Billy Elliot

- *Snatch*
- *Angela's Ashes*
- *Chicken Run*
- *Topsy-Turvy*

Best Director

Bryan Singer - X-Men

- *Michael Mann - The Insider*
- *Ang Lee - Crouching Tiger, Hidden Dragon*
- *Paul Thomas Anderson - Magnolia*
- *Christopher Nolan - Memento*

Best Newcomer

Jamie Bell - Billy Elliot

- *Spike Jonze - Being John Malkovich*
- *Sam Mendes - American Beauty*
- *Sofia Coppola - The Virgin Suicides*
- *Nick Park, Peter Lord - Chicken Run*

Best Film

Gladiator

- *Crouching Tiger, Hidden Dragon*
- *High Fidelity*
- *Magnolia*
- *American Beauty*

Lifetime Achievement Award

Richard Harris

2001 Winners and Nominees

Best Actor

Elijah Wood - The Lord of the Rings: The Fellowship of the Ring

- *Viggo Mortensen - The Lord of the Rings: The Fellowship of the Ring*
- *Benicio del Toro - Traffic*
- *Haley Joel Osment - A.I. Artificial Intelligence*
- *Billy Bob Thornton - The Man Who Wasn't There*

Best Actress

Nicole Kidman - Moulin Rouge

- *Audrey Tautou - Amélie*
- *Renée Zellweger - Bridget Jones's Diary*
- *Nicole Kidman - The Others*
- *Frances O'Connor - A.I. Artificial Intelligence*

Best British Actor

Ewan McGregor - Moulin Rouge

- *Ian McKellen - The Lord of the Rings: The Fellowship of the Ring*
- *Sean Bean - The Lord of the Rings: The Fellowship of the Ring*
- *Hugh Grant - Bridget Jones's Diary*
- *Tim Roth - Planet of the Apes*

Best British Actress

Kate Winslet - Enigma

- *Olivia Williams - Lucky Break*
- *Helena Bonham Carter - Planet of the Apes*
- *Rachel Weisz - The Mummy Returns*
- *Catherine Zeta-Jones - Traffic*

Best British Film

Bridget Jones's Diary

- *The Parole Officer*
- *Mike Basset: England Manager*
- *Luck Break*
- *Enigma*

Best Director

Baz Luhrmann - Moulin Rouge

- *Cameron Crowe - Almost Famous*
- *Steven Spielberg - A.I. Artificial Intelligence*
- *Steven Soderbergh - Traffic*
- *Peter Jackson - The Lord of the Rings: The Fellowship of the Ring*

Best Film

The Lord of the Rings: The Fellowship of the Ring

- *Moulin Rouge*
- *Harry Potter and the Philosopher's Stone*
- *The Others*
- *A.I. Artificial Intelligence*

Best Newcomer

Orlando Bloom - The Lord of the Rings: The Fellowship of the Ring

- *Billy Boyd, Dominic Monaghan - The Lord of the Rings: The Fellowship of the Ring*
- *Sharon Maguire - Bridget Jones's Diary*
- *Daniel Radcliffe, Rupert Grint, Emma Watson - Harry Potter and the Philosopher's Stone*
- *Keira Knightley - The Hole*

Independent Spirit Award

Alejandro Amenábar - The Others

- *Jean-Pierre Jeunet - Amélie*
- *Gael Bernitz - Amores Perros*
- *Terry Zwigoff - Ghost World*

Lifetime Achievement Award

Christopher Lee

2002 Winners and Nominees

Best Actor

Tom Cruise - Minority Report

- *Tom Hanks - Road to Perdition*
- *Viggo Mortensen - The Lord of the Rings: The Two Towers*
- *Mike Myers - Austin Powers in Goldmember*
- *Colin Farrell - Minority Report*

Best Actress

Kirsten Dunst - Spider-Man

- *Hilary Swank - Insomnia*
- *Jennifer Connelly - A Beautiful Mind*
- *Halle Berry - Die Another Day*
- *Miranda Otto - The Lord of the Rings: The Two Towers*

Best British Actor

Hugh Grant - About a Boy

- *Ian McKellen - The Lord of the Rings: The Two Towers*
- *Jude Law - Road to Perdition*
- *Andy Serkis - The Lord of the Rings: The Two Towers*
- *Steve Coogan - 24 Hour Party People*

Best British Actress

Samantha Morton - Minority Report

- *Helen Mirren - Gosford Park*
- *Kelly Macdonald - Gosford Park*
- *Keira Knightley - Bend It Like Beckham*
- *Emily Watson - Red Dragon*

Best British Film

28 Days Later

- *Bend It Like Beckham*
- *About a Boy*
- *24 Hour Party People*
- *The Guru Wikipedia:WikiProject Disambiguation/Fixing links*

Best Director

Steven Spielberg - Minority Report

- *Steven Soderbergh - Ocean's Eleven*
- *M. Night Shyamalan - Signs*
- *Sam Raimi - Spider-Man*
- *Peter Jackson - The Lord of the Rings: The Two Towers*

Best Film

The Lord of the Rings: The Two Towers

- *Spider-Man*
- *Minority Report*
- *Road to Perdition*
- *Die Another Day*

Best Newcomer

Rosamund Pike - Die Another Day

Lifetime Achievement Award

Dustin Hoffman

2003 Winners and Nominees

Best Actor

Johnny Depp - Pirates of the Caribbean: The Curse of the Black Pearl

- *Hugh Jackman - X2: X-Men United*
- *Daniel Day-Lewis - Gangs of New York*
- *Sean Astin - The Lord of the Rings: The Return of the King*
- *Viggo Mortensen - The Lord of the Rings: The Return of the King*

Best Actress

Uma Thurman - Kill Bill, Vol. 1

- *Nicole Kidman - Cold Mountain*
- *Julianne Moore - Far From Heaven*
- *Maggie Gyllenhaal - Secretary*
- *Cate Blanchett - Veronica Guerin*

Best British Actor

Andy Serkis - The Lord of the Rings: The Return of the King

- *Ian McKellen - The Lord of the Rings: The Return of the King*
- *Ewan McGregor - Young Adam*
- *Jude Law - Cold Mountain*
- *Orlando Bloom - The Lord of the Rings: The Return of the King*

Best British Actress

Emma Thompson - Love Actually

- *Helen Mirren - Calendar Girls*
- *Julie Walters - Calendar Girls*
- *Keira Knightley - Pirates of the Caribbean: The Curse of the Black Pearl*
- *Emily Mortimer - Young Adam*

Best British Film

Love Actually

- *Bright Young Things*
- *Calendar Girls*
- *Young Adam*
- *Johnny English*

Best Director

Quentin Tarantino - Kill Bill, Vol. 1

- *Peter Jackson - The Lord of the Rings: The Return of the King*
- *Peter Weir - Master and Commander: The Far Side of the World*
- *Joel Coen, Ethan Coen - Intolerable Cruelty*
- *Anthony Minghella - Cold Mountain*

Best Film

The Lord of the Rings: The Return of the King

- *X2: X-Men United*
- *Kill Bill, Vol. 1*
- *Pirates of the Caribbean: The Curse of the Black Pearl*
- *Cold Mountain*

Best Newcomer

Martine McCutcheon - Love Actually

2006 Winners and Nominees

Best Film

Casino Royale

- *The Departed*
- *Pan's Labyrinth*
- *United 93*
- *Superman Returns*

Best Actor

Daniel Craig - Casino Royale

- *Christian Bale - The Prestige*
- *Leonardo DiCaprio - The Departed*
- *Johnny Depp - Pirates of the Caribbean: Dead Man's Chest*
- *Sacha Baron Cohen - Borat'*

Best Actress

Penélope Cruz - Volver

- *Helen Mirren - The Queen*
- *Keira Knightley - Pirates of the Caribbean: Dead Man's Chest*
- *Reese Witherspoon - Walk the Line*
- *Kate Winslet - Little Children*

Best Director

Christopher Nolan - The Prestige

- *Martin Scorsese - The Departed*
- *Guillermo del Toro - Pan's Labyrinth*
- *Bryan Singer - Superman Returns*
- *George Clooney - Good Night, and Good Luck*

Best Male Newcomer

Brandon Routh - Superman Returns

- Paul Dano - Little Miss Sunshine
- Dominic Cooper - The History Boys
- Alex Pettyfer - Stormbreaker
- Rian Johnson - Brick

Best Thriller

The Departed

- Cache
- Mission: Impossible III
- Munich
- Inside Man

Best British Film

United 93

- The Queen
- Starter for 10
- Confetti
- A Cock and Bull Story

Best Sci-Fi/Fantasy

Pan's Labyrinth

- Children of Men
- Pirates of the Caribbean: Dead Man's Chest
- Superman Returns
- X-Men: The Last Stand

Best Comedy

Little Miss Sunshine

- Borat
- Clerks II
- A Cock and Bull Story
- Nacho Libre

Best Female Newcomer

Eva Green - Casino Royale

- *Rebecca Hall - The Prestige*
- *Abigail Breslin - Little Miss Sunshine*
- *Vera Farmiga - The Departed*
- *Ellen Page - Hard Candy*

2007 Winners and Nominees

Best Film

The Bourne Ultimatum

- *Harry Potter and the Order of the Phoenix*
- *Zodiac*
- *The Assassination of Jesse James by the Coward Robert Ford*
- *Ratatouille*

Best Actor

James McAvoy - Atonement

- *Gerard Butler - 300*
- *Daniel Radcliffe - Harry Potter and the Order of the Phoenix*
- *Simon Pegg - Hot Fuzz*
- *Matt Damon - The Bourne Ultimatum*

Best Actress

Keira Knightley - Atonement

- *Cate Blanchett - Elizabeth: The Golden Age*
- *Angelina Jolie - A Mighty Heart*
- *Katherine Heigl - Knocked Up*
- *Emma Watson - Harry Potter and the Order of the Phoenix*

Best Director

David Yates - Harry Potter and the Order of the Phoenix

- Joe Wright - Atonement
- Paul Greengrass - The Bourne Ultimatum
- David Fincher - Zodiac
- Hot Fuzz - Edgar Wright

Best Soundtrack

Control

- Atonement
- Once
- Hairspray
- Harry Potter and the Order of the Phoenix

Best Thriller

American Gangster

- The Bourne Ultimatum
- Disturbia
- Zodiac
- Eastern Promises

Best British Film

Atonement

- Sunshine
- This Is England
- Control
- Hot Fuzz

Best Newcomer

Sam Riley - Control

- Saoirse Ronan - Atonement
- Gemma Arterton - St Trinian's
- Shia LaBeouf - Transformers
- Thomas Turgoose - This Is England

Best Sci-Fi/Fantasy

Stardust

- *300*
- *Harry Potter and the Order of the Phoenix*
- *Sunshine*
- *Transformers*

Best Comedy

Hot Fuzz

- *Knocked Up*
- *Superbad*
- *Run Fatboy Run*
- *Ratatouille*

Past winners

- Empire Awards 1998
- Empire Awards 2004
- Empire Awards 2005
- Empire Awards 2009
- Empire Awards 2010

Article Sources and Contributors

Christopher Nolan *Source*: http://en.wikipedia.org/?oldid=390611790 *Contributors*: -5-

Emma Thomas *Source*: http://en.wikipedia.org/?oldid=390214036 *Contributors*: 1 anonymous edits

Jonathan Nolan *Source*: http://en.wikipedia.org/?oldid=389650772 *Contributors*: -5-

Superhero film *Source*: http://en.wikipedia.org/?oldid=388301654 *Contributors*: -5-

Neo-noir *Source*: http://en.wikipedia.org/?oldid=389829026 *Contributors*: 1 anonymous edits

Thriller (genre) *Source*: http://en.wikipedia.org/?oldid=388893298 *Contributors*: Shirt58

Christian Bale *Source*: http://en.wikipedia.org/?oldid=390642247 *Contributors*: Jack Merridew

Morgan Freeman *Source*: http://en.wikipedia.org/?oldid=390627749 *Contributors*: Yinzland

Michael Caine *Source*: http://en.wikipedia.org/?oldid=390475439 *Contributors*: Rossrs

Memento (film) *Source*: http://en.wikipedia.org/?oldid=388312016 *Contributors*: 1 anonymous edits

Batman Begins *Source*: http://en.wikipedia.org/?oldid=390526899 *Contributors*: Allmightyduck

Insomnia (2002 film) *Source*: http://en.wikipedia.org/?oldid=389641652 *Contributors*: Wolverine7044

Following *Source*: http://en.wikipedia.org/?oldid=390672795 *Contributors*: CapitalLetterBeginning

The Prestige (film) *Source*: http://en.wikipedia.org/?oldid=388558012 *Contributors*: 1 anonymous edits

The Dark Knight (film) *Source*: http://en.wikipedia.org/?oldid=390429611 *Contributors*: FrankRizzo2006

Inception (film) *Source*: http://en.wikipedia.org/?oldid=390558108 *Contributors*:

American Film Institute *Source*: http://en.wikipedia.org/?oldid=390186204 *Contributors*: 1 anonymous edits

International Film Festival Rotterdam *Source*: http://en.wikipedia.org/?oldid=359325021 *Contributors*: Pjoef

Broadcast Film Critics Association Award *Source*: http://en.wikipedia.org/?oldid=332552141 *Contributors*: 1 anonymous edits

Independent Spirit Awards *Source*: http://en.wikipedia.org/?oldid=369819576 *Contributors*: Martarius

Sundance Film Festival *Source*: http://en.wikipedia.org/?oldid=390664184 *Contributors*: Martarius

Saturn Award *Source*: http://en.wikipedia.org/?oldid=388274702 *Contributors*:

Empire Awards *Source*: http://en.wikipedia.org/?oldid=387805396 *Contributors*: Fernandosmission

Image Sources, Licenses and Contributors

CPSIA information can be obtained at www.ICGtesting.com
Printed in the USA
BVOW031137200113

311105BV00005B/160/P